SPECIESISM

D1570470

SPECIESISM

JOAN DUNAYER

RYCE PUBLISHING
Derwood, Maryland

2004

RYCE PUBLISHING
7806 Fairborn Court
Derwood, Maryland 20855-2227
www.rycepublishing.com
info@rycepublishing.com

Publisher's Cataloging-in-Publication Data

Dunayer, Joan
Speciesism / Joan Dunayer;
   p.   cm.
   Includes bibliographical references and index.
ISBN 0-9706475-6-5
   1. Speciesism
   2. Animal rights
   3. Animal rights movement
   I. Title
HV4708.D868 2004
179'.3—dc22
Library of Congress Control Number: 2004093745

Printed in the United States of America

For all nonhuman animals

Contents

Acknowledgments

In *Speciesism* I build on the work of other animal rights theorists, such as Paola Cavalieri, Gary Francione, David Nibert, Evelyn Pluhar, James Rachels, Tom Regan, Bernard Rollin, Steve Sapontzis, and Peter Singer. My intellectual debt to Francione, Regan, and Sapontzis is especially large.

Eric Dunayer generously expended considerable time and effort obtaining and sending me numerous source materials. A veterinary toxicologist, Eric read the manuscript and lent scientific expertise. His editorial advice further improved the book.

Lawyer and animal rights advocate Sean Day answered questions about the law and gave helpful feedback on *Speciesism*'s law chapters. I also benefited from discussing abolitionist and "welfarist" advocacy with Sean.

Lee Hall, legal director of Friends of Animals, provided useful publications, read the manuscript at different stages in its development, advised on matters of law, and made many invaluable suggestions. Her comments encouraged me, challenged me, and, when I thought that I had done my best, prompted me to do better.

To everyone who works for nonhuman emancipation: thank you. No cause is more important or more just.

Preface on Language

Words have political effect. They can foster oppression or liberation, prejudice or respect. Just as sexist language denigrates or discounts females, speciesist language denigrates or discounts nonhumans; it legitimizes their abuse. Throughout this book I've painstakingly tried to avoid speciesist, sexist, and otherwise-biased language.

In keeping with scientific fact, I include humans in "animals," "mammals," "primates," and "apes." Usage that excludes humans from animalkind maintains a moral divide between humans and other animals. Rather than speaking of "humans and animals," I speak of "humans and nonhumans."

Even the word *nonhuman* divides all animals into two, seemingly opposed categories: humans and everyone else. With equal validity we could categorize all animals as robins and nonrobins. Still, *nonhuman animal* (*nonhuman* for short) avoids limiting animals to nonhumans. Also, for now we must speak in terms of humans and all other animals because all other animals lack legal rights. Some people contend that the prefix *non-* automatically assigns a negative valuation. To the contrary, words such as *noncombatant*, *nonsexist*, and *nonpartisan* are neutral or positive.

Because the category "animals" includes humans, I use *nonhuman rights* when referring to the rights only of nonhumans and *animal rights* when referring to the rights of all sentient beings (including humans), as in *animal rights movement*. Animal rights advocates don't seek to limit rights to nonhumans; they seek to expand fundamental rights from humans to other animals.

Currently, biologists classify as "animals" some organisms that lack a nervous system and are therefore extremely unlikely to be sentient (capable of experiencing). In moral terms these organisms belong with other insentient things, such as bacteria, rather than with human and nonhuman beings. For this reason I don't include them in "animals." (Biologists themselves may eventually place these anomalous organisms in a separate taxonomic category.) When I speak of "animals" or "nonhumans," I mean sentient beings, who possess a nervous system. Because all sentient organisms are conscious beings, unique individuals, and, in a moral sense, persons, I sometimes refer to nonhumans as "beings," "individuals," and "persons."

My pronoun use acknowledges nonhuman consciousness and individuality. Every sentient being is "who" (not "that" or "which"), "some*one*" (not "some*thing*"). According to current scientific knowledge, every animal is male, female, or hermaphroditic, so I use *he*, *she*, or *she/he* (alternatively *he/she*) for any specific nonhuman individual.

Many grammarians object to combining *they* with a grammatically singular pronoun such as *anyone*, *everyone*, or *someone*. However, common practice long has paired grammatically singular pronouns with plural ones. "Someone left their umbrella" sounds natural and familiar. When an indefinite pronoun refers to an individual of unknown sex, I use *they* whether the individual is human or nonhuman. In fact, I use a plural pronoun for any unspecified individual of unknown sex (as in "Whenever I see a turtle on the road, I move *them* to safety"). This usage avoids clumsy *he or she* and *she or he*, which interfere with a sense of person, an individual with one continuing identity. Similarly, I use *she/he* and *he/she* only for hermaphrodites.

To remind readers that any group of nonhumans consists of multiple individuals, I often use uncommon (but accepted) plural forms that end in *s*: *fishes* rather than *fish*, *squids* rather than *squid*, *minks* rather than *mink*. As noted in *The Merriam-Webster Concise Handbook for Writers*, hunters, fishers, and trappers generally refer to their victims with plurals identical to singular forms: two "quail," three "trout," four "beaver."[1] Such usage blurs the victims together, de-emphasizing their individual sufferings and deaths.

Euphemisms further disguise speciesist abuse. I've worked hard to avoid them. I don't sanitize flesh as "meat," cow skin as "leather," vivisection as "biomedical research," or food-industry captivity and slaughter as "animal agriculture." Unduly positive words appear only in quotation marks: a "purebred" dog is inbred; "farmed" animals are confined and killed; "shelters" that kill healthy, homeless animals are adoption-and-killing facilities. "Aquariums" and "marine parks" imprison aquatic animals, so I call them aquaprisons. Some people have objected that *prison* implies guilt, and nonhuman captives aren't guilty of anything. Political prisoners aren't guilty. Nonhumans are political prisoners. The politics is speciesism. In legal terms, nonhumans are falsely imprisoned.

Like euphemisms, terms that demean nonhumans promote speciesist practices. For example, *livestock* and *wildlife conservation* reduce nonhumans to commodities—to "stock" or a "conserved" resource. Saying that animals are "grown," "farmed," or genetically "engineered" equates them with plants or machines. In *Speciesism* I've flagged such denigrating language with quotation marks.

I've also flagged oxymorons. With regard to human breeding of nonhumans, there's no such thing as "responsible breeding." Breeding other animals for human pleasure or use exploits nonhumans and violates their autonomy. We have no moral right to genetically manipulate other beings or manufacture their existence for our purposes. Similarly, "humane slaughter" doesn't exist: slaughtering innocents is inhumane, whether or not the killing method is less cruel than other methods.

Many category labels applied to nonhumans legitimize speciesist exploitation by making it seem natural and inevitable: *game animals*, *veal calves*, *lab animals*... I reject such labels, which suggest that victimization arises from the nature of the victims rather than the perceptions and choices of their abusers. Deer needn't be hunted, calves needn't be killed for their flesh, and rats—including those bred for vivisection—needn't be vivisected. The victimizer, not the victim, causes victimization.

As the author of a book on speciesist language (*Animal Equality: Language and Liberation*), I've closely examined the connections between standard English usage and speciesist abuse.[2] The way we speak about other animals is inseparable from the way we treat them. Along with our actions, our words must accord them full consideration and respect.

1

Speciesism Defined

Whenever you see a bird in a cage, fish in a tank, or nonhuman mammal on a chain, you're seeing speciesism. If you believe that a bee or frog has less right to life and liberty than a chimpanzee or human, or you consider humans superior to other animals, you subscribe to speciesism. If you visit aquaprisons and zoos, attend circuses that include "animal acts," wear nonhuman skin or hair, or eat flesh, eggs, or cow-milk products, you practice speciesism. If you campaign for more-"humane" slaughter of chickens or less-cruel confinement of pigs, you perpetuate speciesism.

What, exactly, is speciesism? In 1970 psychologist Richard Ryder coined the word *speciesism* in a leaflet of the same name. Although he didn't explicitly define the term, he indicated that speciesists draw a sharp moral distinction between humans and all other animals. They fail to "extend our concern about elementary rights to the non-human animals."[1]

With the 1975 publication of *Animal Liberation*, philosopher Peter Singer brought the concept of speciesism widespread attention. He defined speciesism as

> a prejudice or attitude of bias toward the interests of members of one's own species and against those of members of other species.[2]

That definition falls short. Consider a comparable definition of racism:

> a prejudice or attitude of bias toward the interests of members of one's own race and against those of members of other races.

Yes, bias toward whites and against all other races is racist. However, bias toward whites and against *any number* of other races also is racist. All of the following are racist: prejudice against only Semites; prejudice against only Africans, Native Americans, and Australian Aborigines; prejudice against everyone *except* whites and Asians. Analogously, bias toward humans and against any number of other species (say, all rats and mice) is speciesist. So is bias toward humans and *toward* any other species (e.g., chimpanzees and gorillas).

In a 2003 article, Singer defined speciesism more narrowly than in *Animal Liberation*:

> the idea that it is justifiable to give preference to beings simply on the grounds that they are members of the species *Homo sapiens*.[3]

By "preference" Singer means greater moral consideration. This definition of speciesism is more inadequate than his earlier one. Now, in addition to limiting speciesism to bias toward only one species (our own), Singer limits it to bias *simply* on the grounds of species membership.

Again, consider a comparable definition of racism:

> the idea that it is justifiable to give preference to certain individuals simply on the grounds that they are white.

Isn't it racist to give greater moral consideration to whites on *any* grounds, such as their generally having lighter skin or a higher standard of living than nonwhites?

A parallel definition of sexism might help:

> the idea that it is justifiable to give preference to certain individuals simply on the grounds that they are male.

It's sexist to give men greater moral consideration than women on *any* grounds, such as men's generally being more muscular or scoring higher on tests of spatial orientation. Likewise, it's speciesist to give humans greater moral consideration than nonhumans on *any* grounds, such as humans' generally possessing written language and engaging in more tool use.

Clearly, Singer's definition of speciesism is overly narrow in two ways: (1) it limits speciesism to bias in favor of only one species; (2) it limits speciesism to bias based solely on species membership.

Like Singer, philosopher Tom Regan defines speciesism as giving "privileged moral status" to all humans and no nonhumans.[4] Again, it's also speciesist to morally privilege all humans and only *some* nonhumans. To me, the speciesism of privileging mammals and birds is as obvious as the racism of privileging Europeans and Asians or the sexism of privileging men and exceptionally masculine women.

Also like Singer, Regan further defines speciesism as "assigning greater weight to the interests of human beings just because they are human."[5] This bears repeating: It's racist to give greater weight to the interests of whites than nonwhites, sexist to give greater weight to the interests of males than females, and speciesist to give greater weight to the interests of humans than nonhumans for *any* reason.

According to Singer and Regan, someone is not speciesist if they give full moral consideration to *any* nonhumans—for example, those who most resemble humans in appearance, observed behavior, and apparent cognition. Giving full moral consideration to whites and mulattos, but not blacks, extends equality to some nonwhites but still is racist. Giving full moral consideration to men and only exceptionally masculine women extends equality to some women but still is sexist. Likewise, giving full moral consideration to humans and only some nonhumans—such as other apes—extends equality to some nonhumans but still is speciesist.

Philosopher Paola Cavalieri comments that *speciesism* could "be used to describe any form of discrimination based on species."[6] For the reasons I've given, that's how *speciesism* should be used. Unfortunately, Cavalieri adopts the standard Singer–Regan definition. Her stated reason is weak: The moral line that has been drawn between humans and all other animals is "so salient" that speciesism has "come to be seen as practically interchangeable with the notion of human chauvinism."[7] During black enslavement in America, someone could have said with equal validity, "The moral line that has been drawn between whites and nonwhites is so salient that racism has come to be seen as practically interchangeable with the notion of white supremacy." The fact remains that any discrimination based on race is racist, whether the discrimination is against all nonwhites, some nonwhites, all non-Asians, all whites, or any other racial group(s). Whether or not speciesism and human chauvinism have "come to be seen as practically interchangeable," they *aren't* interchangeable. Human chauvinism is one type of speciesism.

According to Singer, it isn't speciesist to believe that "there are morally relevant differences between human beings and other animals that entitle us to give more weight to the interests of humans."[8] It *is* speciesist. There are no such differences, just as there are no differences between whites and nonwhites or males and females that entitle us to give more weight to the interests of whites or males.

To warrant full and equal moral consideration, someone need only be sentient, possessing some form of consciousness. Why is it wrong to torture or murder humans, force them to labor, harm them in experiments, or imprison them for life when they've committed no crime? Why is it wrong to deprive humans of well-being or life except under extraordinary circumstances, such as those necessitating self-defense? Because most humans reason abstractly, possess verbal language, use technology, and have social ties? No. After all, it's wrong (and illegal) to torment or kill humans, such as unloved infants, who lack some or all of those characteristics. Treating humans in particular ways is wrong because humans are sentient. They experience. Harming them causes them to suffer. Killing them deprives them of any further experience. The same is true of all other animals.

As Singer would agree, it's speciesist to deny nonhumans moral consideration. However, it's also speciesist to accord them *less* consideration than humans, just as it's racist or sexist to accord nonwhites or females less consideration than whites or males.

As Singer also would agree, it's speciesist to weigh trivial human interests more heavily than significant nonhuman interests. However, it's also speciesist to weigh *significant* human interests more heavily than equally significant nonhuman ones.

Like racists and sexists, speciesists rationalize discriminatory treatment. And what *is* discriminatory treatment? Giving more weight to the interests of some than others—precisely what Singer attempts to rationalize. On the one hand, Singer defines speciesism as "bias toward the interests" of humans. On the other, he claims that it isn't speciesist to give "more weight to the interests of humans." The self-contradiction arises because Singer himself is trying to defend a breed of speciesism. When we defend speciesist ideology, we legitimize the actions that flow from that ideology.

Sociologist David Nibert has described speciesism as an ideology "created and promulgated to legitimate killing and exploitation of other animals."[9] His definition includes cause and effect. In his view, human oppression of nonhumans came first; prejudice followed. However, someone could argue the opposite: Oppression couldn't have occurred without some feeling of entitlement, some sense that it was morally acceptable to exploit other animals; except when humans act reflexively, they decide to do something before they do it. The fact is, it's impossible to determine which came first: oppression or its psychological justification, speciesist actions or speciesist attitudes. Still, Nibert makes an important point: Speciesist attitudes and practices are inextricably linked. They continually feed each other.

Speciesism entails both arrogance and injustice: human conceit and an accompanying disposition to abuse nonhumans. Speciesists devalue nonhuman interests because they devalue nonhumans, whom they regard as inferior, less deserving of consideration. The assumption of human superiority lies at speciesism's core. Human self-aggrandizement manifests as disrespect (or less respect) for other animals.

In sum, speciesism is both an attitude and a form of oppression. Viewing humans as superior to other animals, speciesists weigh human interests more heavily than equally vital or more-vital nonhuman interests. It's speciesist to exclude *any* nonhuman being from full and equal moral consideration for *any* reason.

This, then, is the definition of speciesism that I'll develop and defend throughout this book:

> a failure, in attitude or practice, to accord any nonhuman being equal consideration and respect.

OLD SPECIESISM

2

Old-Speciesist Philosophy

Old-fashioned speciesists—whom I'll call "old-speciesists"—don't believe that any nonhumans should have legal rights or receive as much moral consideration as humans. By "legal rights" I mean basic rights, such as rights to life and liberty, currently accorded only to humans (legal "persons").

Old-speciesists see nonhumans and humans as fundamentally different. The common expression "the sanctity of human life" conveys their attitude: human life is special.

Old-speciesists regard nonhumans as of little or no importance except in relation to humans. They consider it acceptable to kill and otherwise harm nonhumans to serve human ends. In their view, nonhumans exist for human pleasure and use, constituting a single exploitable group.

"I Don't Care"

To some old-speciesists, humans warrant exceptional moral consideration simply because they're human. We belong to the right group: *Homo sapiens*.

Morally, viewing individuals solely in terms of their group makes no sense, because experience takes place at the level of the individual. The wrongness of torturing a human doesn't arise from their being a member of the human species. After all, a human can't be tortured if they're brain-dead. For torture to occur, the individual must be sentient. Similarly, the wrongness of finding an infant guilty of murder doesn't lie in their being human but in their not knowing right from wrong. Nor is it morally *acceptable* to harm a human simply because they're human. Instead, the context—for example, self-defense—must justify the harm. Then, why is it acceptable to harm a nonhuman simply because they're nonhuman?

Limiting rights to members of one species is no more logical or fair than limiting rights to members of one race or sex. Declaring humans uniquely entitled to rights begs the question "*Why* are humans uniquely entitled to rights?"

In many cases the answer is sheer favoritism: "I just care more about humans, and I don't see anything wrong with that." Everyone is entitled to their personal preferences. However, we're *not* entitled to translate our preferences into privileges for some at others' expense. Most humans favor members of their own family, social circle, and race. Many whites don't care about blacks. Blacks still need legal rights. In fact, they need legal rights all the more, to protect them from racist preferences. Analogously, many humans don't care about nonhumans, who need legal rights to protect them from speciesist preferences. Only unjust humans claim that basic rights should be limited to members of *their* family, race, or other group—including species. Equitable laws counter, rather than institutionalize, bias.

Like other bigotries, speciesism is a failure to empathize with those outside one's group. Few humans, including those guilty of crimes against humanity, are totally incapable of compassion or love. But many deny full (or any) moral consideration to humans they see as outsiders, such as foreigners and people who don't share their religious beliefs. Nazis don't extend moral consideration to Jews. Ku Klux Klan members don't extend it to blacks. In parallel, old-speciesists don't extend it to nonhumans. From human genocide to nonhuman vivisection, systematic abuse requires absence of empathy.

Having shot a deer in the hip, a bowhunter complained, "You should have seen the bastard take off. Lost an arrow."[1] Pig enslavers castrate piglets without anesthetic. According to an industry article, this can be "harrowing"—for the castrator.[2] When a power failure severed the air supply to 130 mice confined in sealed chambers, killing all but three, the vivisector experimenting on the mice remarked, "I don't think we have much choice but to laugh and start over."[3]

In general, old-speciesists simply disregard the myriad nonhumans whom humans intentionally hurt and kill. Who cares if millions of mice and rats are vivisected? They're "only rodents." What does it matter if billions of chickens live in misery until they die in pain and fear? They're "just chickens." They aren't human, so they don't count. Victimizers lack empathy for their victims, but absence of empathy doesn't *justify* victimization, whether the victims are human or nonhuman.

"The Bible Says So"

Many Christians believe that nonhumans exist for human use because the Bible says so. As expressed by one man, "God put us in charge over animals."[4]

Saying that humans are entitled to dominion over nonhumans doesn't make it so. (Some sexist men likewise claim that men are entitled to dominion over women.) Humans wrote the Bible, so it isn't surprising that the Bible glorifies humans and gives them license to exploit other animals. Given that the Bible sanctions *human* enslavement, we hardly can expect it to censure nonhuman enslavement. In addition to being sexist, tribalistic, and otherwise biased against particular human groups, the Bible is speciesist.

Genuine arguments are based on evidence and reasoning. People who look to the Bible for their beliefs have a fundamentally irrational worldview. Christian old-speciesists have absorbed the human-aggrandizing myths that "Creation" culminated in humans, "God" made humans in "His" image, and Jesus (human and male) was divine. In Christianity, humans are more god-like than other animals. They're God's "children," whereas other animals are merely His "creatures." Extremely human-centered and hierarchical, Christian doctrine is incompatible with animal equality.

At best, old-speciesists who base their beliefs on the Bible have some sense of noblesse oblige toward nonhumans. They feel a condescending benevolence but not respect. They see other animals as inferiors in need of control or care rather than equals entitled to justice. In their paternalistic and proprietary view, God the Father gave nonhumans to his children, humans. Nonhumans are human property, the opposite of individuals with rights.

Christian old-speciesists display Christianity's bias against non-human animals. Like the Bible, they maintain a sharp moral divide between humans and all other animals. (They would say "humans and animals," which is logically equivalent to "blacks and humans" or "women and humans.")

Many religious speciesists deny human–nonhuman kinship. It discomforts them to think of *Homo sapiens* as one animal species among millions and downright alarms them to see themselves as animals, primates, and apes.

Nonhuman apes are more closely related to humans than to monkeys. If nonhuman apes and monkeys are primates, so are we. Biologists now classify gibbons, orangutans, gorillas, bonobos, chimpanzees, *and humans* as apes. African nonhuman apes (gorillas, bonobos, and chimpanzees) share a more recent common ancestor with humans than with Asian nonhuman apes (gibbons and orangutans). If gorillas and orangutans are apes, we are too. Genetically, bonobos and chimpanzees are closer to humans than to either orangutans or gorillas. They share about 96.4 percent of their genes with orangutans, 97.7 percent with gorillas, and 98.4 percent with humans. We belong in the same genus (*Homo* or *Pan*) as bonobos and chimpanzees. But old-speciesists prefer to think of humans in splendid isolation.

Having failed to evolve beyond the myths of former centuries, many old-speciesists don't believe in evolution. As expressed by one sport hunter, evolution indicates human "kindredship" with "animals," so anyone who believes in evolution could conclude that killing nonhumans "constitutes murder." He's decided not to believe in evolution.[5] That way he can have his gun and use it, too.

Anxious to maintain feelings of superiority and preserve a human monopoly on moral and legal rights, old-speciesists grossly exaggerate human uniqueness. To varying degrees, all animal species overlap physically and mentally. At the same time, each animal is unique.

"They Aren't Individuals"

Speciesism's hallmark is denial of nonhuman individuality. Old-speciesists see a nonhuman animal as some*thing* rather than some*one*, an insentient "it" rather than a thinking, feeling individual.

The failure to see individuals *as* individuals is the essence of all bigotries. White racists see an individual black as an embodiment of race; sexist men see an individual woman primarily as female. Analogously, speciesists think of cheetahs and flies as generic, as if all cheetahs or flies were the same.

To large extent, nonhuman individuals lack basic rights because speciesists don't think of them as individuals. This is especially true of speciesists who think mainly in terms of group membership rather than individual characteristics.

"Animals are not correctly thought of as individuals," a hunter has stated.[6] If it isn't correct to think of nonhuman animals as individuals, then it isn't correct to think of human animals as individuals either. In reality, there's no generic hamster, ant, stingray, or crane, any more than there's a generic human. However inbred for genetic uniformity, nonhumans are born with unique physical and mental characteristics. Unique life experiences further shape them as individuals. Cloned nonhumans are no less individual than human identical twins, who also develop from one split embryo. Both physically and mentally, all sentient beings are unique.

But speciesists think of nonhuman individuals as exploitable types. A turkey is "poultry"; a pig is "livestock"; a rat is a "lab rat." Comparable language would declare a bank teller a "bank human," as if that person were nothing but a member of a particular work force, essentially like everyone else who works in a bank.

From aquaprison directors to food-industry enslavers, speciesist exploiters commonly say that they "replace" nonhumans who die or are of no further use. They speak of nonhumans as interchangeable: "replacement boars," "replacement cows," "replacement hens." One by one, billions upon billions, nonhumans are killed without compunction, provided that others of their species remain available for future killing.

Over the years, 38 of my companions have been rats. Each of them had a distinct personality. Yet, a vivisector of rats has called unique rat personalities "a strange concept."[7] Similarly, a vivisector of cats has stated that cats don't have personalities.[8] Anyone who ever has had a cat companion knows otherwise.

Many speciesists think of nonhumans as mere species samples: "specimens." Vivisectors and their assistants often address nonhumans by the name of their species or other animal group. In a video filmed undercover at a product-testing lab, a technician applies deodorant concentrate to a rabbit's shaved skin. The rabbit struggles, and the technician snaps, "Cut it out, rabbit."[9]

Linguistically, speciesists commonly confuse individuals with species. Hunters and fishers incorrectly speak of killing species rather than individuals. "I've killed eight species of deer," hunters boast, rather than "deer of eight species." (Fortunately, individual hunters don't single-handedly kill off entire species, although some have tried.)

Whenever the media report that someone has killed "an endangered animal" or "an endangered species," they too confuse an individual with a species. *Any* animal threatened with a gun or arrow is endangered. Hunters kill *members* of endangered species. Conversely, animals who are personally safe are not endangered, even if they belong to an endangered species.

To speciesists, most nonhumans matter only at the level of species or subspecies. The director of New York City's zoological society has remarked, "The things we are exhibiting [in zoos] are disappearing."[10] The "things" in zoo enclosures are individuals, not species. However, the standard zoo sign identifies an enclosure's inmates by species, describes not the imprisoned individuals but their free-living counterparts, and does so in collective terms such as weight range, average or maximum life span, possible diets and habitats, and the species' geographic extent and population status (especially if the species is endangered). If you were caged in typical zoo fashion, the sign on your cage would read "Human" and describe *Homo sapiens* as a whole.

Along with "wildlife conservationists," many self-styled environmentalists view most or all nonhumans strictly in terms of their species membership. Concerned only that species remain viable, they regard individual nonhumans as expendable. They value members of endangered species more than members of highly populous species. To be consistent (and nonspeciesist), these "environmentalists" would have to value the life of an Atlantic salmon more than the life of a human because, in environmental terms, there are too few Atlantic salmons and far too many humans. But most so-called environmentalists make an exception for humans, even though human overpopulation causes environmental devastation and humans are the chief destroyers of species and ecosystems. Ironically, the primary cause of the species extinctions that environmentalists bewail is the very speciesism to which they subscribe: the belief that humans, being the best and most important creatures, are entitled to capture other animals, genetically manipulate them, kill them, and appropriate their land. Like all other speciesists, most environmentalists apply a double standard.

"Humans Have Unique Characteristics"

Many old-speciesists claim that one or more characteristics entitle humans alone to moral and legal rights. These speciesists don't consider whether or not a particular human or nonhuman individual actually possesses the characteristic(s). Instead they deny rights to all nonhumans on one of two grounds: (1) most humans possess the characteristic(s), whereas most nonhumans don't; (2) most humans possess the characteristic(s) to a greater degree than most nonhumans.

This stance is neither logical nor fair. Giving all humans and no nonhumans rights would be justifiable only if (1) *all* humans and *no* nonhumans possessed the required characteristic(s) and (2) the characteristic(s) had moral relevance. In reality, with regard to all proposed characteristics, some humans lack them and at least some nonhumans possess them. More importantly, sentience is the only valid criterion for basic rights.

A Soul

Attempting to justify cow slaughter, a kosher slaughterer claimed that only humans possess a soul.[11] The soul criterion is the exception to the rule that old-speciesists ignore nonhumans who possess (and humans who lack) characteristics deemed necessary for rights. Many religious people believe that all humans and no nonhumans possess a soul. They can't be proven wrong. However, the claim that *anyone* possesses a soul lacks the support of evidence or logic.

Also, the soul issue isn't relevant to basic rights. Why on Earth (or beyond) would it be more justifiable to inflict suffering and death on someone who doesn't have a soul than on someone who does? (In earlier eras, Christians frequently tortured or killed humans in an alleged effort to *save* their souls.)

Anyone who believes that an afterlife compensates humans, but not nonhumans, for undeserved suffering should find nonhuman suffering more appalling than human suffering. Anyone who believes that only humans experience life after death should find nonhuman death more tragic than human death. The soul criterion makes no sense.

An Ability to Enter into Contracts

Nonhumans shouldn't have legal rights, other old-speciesists claim, because they can't enter into social contracts and fulfill responsibilities. Infants, young children, and numerous adult humans with permanent mental disabilities can't enter into contracts either. They can't negotiate agreements or understand accountability. They're the very humans most vulnerable to abuse and, therefore, most in need of legal protection. And the law *does* protect them.

The contract argument is fundamentally inconsistent. If an inability to make contracts banishes all nonhumans from the realm of rights, it must banish many humans as well.

The contract argument is an incoherent excuse for continuing to deny rights to nonhumans. In effect, it's little more than "Might makes right": Humans have the power and ability to make laws, so they're entitled to make them solely for their own benefit. Again, only some humans have the power and ability to make laws. If they're compassionate and just, they make laws that also protect humans who can't enter into contracts. Compassion and justice similarly require laws that protect nonhumans.

However belatedly (and still not universally), male lawmakers have extended basic legal rights to women. In the United States, in South Africa, and elsewhere, white lawmakers have extended legal rights to blacks. Humans likewise should extend legal rights to nonhumans. Yes, women and blacks can participate in lawmaking, whereas nonhumans can't; but many humans with mental disabilities can't participate either.

The contract argument reflects a fundamental misunderstanding of nonhuman rights. Animal rights advocates don't seek some kind of contract *between* humans and nonhumans. They seek a contract among humans, a legally binding agreement that nonhumans have basic rights—for example, to life and liberty.

Laws restrict human behavior. Animal rights advocates want laws that will prohibit humans from exploiting and otherwise harming nonhumans. They don't seek to protect nonhumans within human society. They seek to protect nonhumans *from* human society. The goal is an end to nonhumans' "domestication" and other forced "participation" in human society. Nonhumans should be allowed to live free in natural environments, forming their own societies.

The laws that currently oppress nonhumans are contracts among humans. No speciesist argues that *those* laws should be void because nonhumans had no part in framing them.

Nonhumans' current property status is a social and legal construct. Lawmakers have characterized lethal trapping of nonhumans as lawful killing. They could just as easily characterize it as murder.

Humans have taken unfair advantage of nonhumans' lack of political power. Instead of using their lawmaking ability to extend justice to all, they've used it to exclude nonhumans from justice.

Making sentience the sole criterion for legal rights not only would protect nonhumans; it also would affirm the rights of the most vulnerable humans. If mallards and butterflies had legal rights, the rights of autistic and senile humans would be more, not less, secure. Opponents often claim that nonhuman rights would diminish human rights. To the contrary, laws that protect the most vulnerable beings protect us all.

A Life of More Value

"Every human life is more important than every nonhuman one because human life has more value to *others*," some old-speciesists claim. Whether "has more value to others" means "is valued more by others" or "confers more benefit on others," that claim is false.

Some humans are valued by no one. Many nonhumans are greatly valued by their kin or other companions. For example, geese and wolves are loved by their mates.

If the extent to which someone is valued determined their legal rights, loved humans would have more rights than unloved ones. Also, the law would protect a cat loved by a large human family, or bear cubs loved by their mother, more than it protects an unloved hermit or human orphan. Whether or not they're valued by others, humans possess legal rights. So should nonhumans.

As for benefiting others: most humans probably have little or negative value to most other humans, especially those with whom they compete for jobs and resources. The vast majority of the world's living beings are nonhumans. To most of them, humans have highly negative value. After all, humans routinely harm other animals, both directly and indirectly—for example, by enslaving them, slaughtering them, and polluting, clear-cutting, or otherwise destroying their habitats.

If many humans provide care to other individuals and otherwise contribute to their communities, so do many nonhumans. Unlike most humans, free-living nonhumans also contribute to their ecosystems. For example, insects of numerous species pollinate a host of plants that provide food to countless other animals (including humans). In terms of their lives' objective value to most other beings, humans probably rank lowest of all animals.

To old-speciesists, nonhumans must justify their existence by proving useful to humans; in contrast, some or all humans have inherent value. Old-speciesists have a rights view of at least some humans but a utilitarian view of nonhumans.

In zoos and aquaprisons, nonhumans are displayed objects, "exhibits" in a "collection." In vivisection they're research "tools." According to some speciesists, humans are entitled to make virtually any use of nonhumans whom they breed. "Nude mice did not exist in nature," a vivisector has stated. "We have created them for our use and are, therefore, justified in using them accordingly."[12] No human ever has "created" any nonhuman animal. Even if humans did create a nonhuman, they wouldn't be justified in exploiting that individual. Like nonhumans, all humans are born as a consequence of others' actions. We don't allow physicians and technicians who perform *in vitro* fertilization to wield absolute power over the humans who result. We don't permit parents to enslave or murder their children.

Old-speciesists categorize nonhumans as useful, superfluous, or troublesome (like toasters, extra electric outlets, or potholes) and label them accordingly. *Furbearer* tags animals potential pelts. *Game animal* designates them hunting targets. *Dairy cow* characterizes cows as producers of milk for human consumption. (However inbred and enslaved, a cow doesn't produce milk for humans. She produces it for her calf.) To fishers, caught but unwanted fishes are "trash." To the egg industry, male chicks are "waste"; they're ground up alive or tossed into trash bags, where they suffocate. What's true of all "trash" animals is the way they're viewed and treated: like garbage. Humans routinely kill unwanted dogs and cats; horses and grey-hounds too slow, old, or injured to race; hens and queen honeybees whose egg production has declined; and other "useless" nonhumans. Humans casually murder spiders, silverfishes, and other "creepy" in-vertebrates who are harmless (or beneficial) to humans. They try to exterminate so-called varmints, vermin, and pests. Despite human overpopulation and crowding, only nonhumans are said to "infest" an area. Humans continually encroach on nonhuman territory and condemn to death the "nuisance animals" who dare to remain. If death sentences were handed out with equal alacrity to humans who annoy, inconvenience, or compete with others, few of us would re-main alive.

There's no objective sense in which human life has more value than nonhuman life. People who claim that human life has more value simply express their own preference: *they* value human life more.

A Greater Capacity to Suffer

Many old-speciesists contend that nonhumans have less capacity to suffer than humans and therefore less need of legal protection. Abus-ers of nonhumans habitually discount nonhuman pain. Vivisectors rarely give their victims pain-killers, even after major surgery.[13] Humans find being shot in the chest excruciating. According to a hunter, shooting a deer in the lungs causes no more pain than a bee sting.[14] Cattle have such sensitive skin that they feel a fly alight. Yet, a flesh-industry textbook states that cattle branded with a red-hot iron feel only "some discomfort."[15] In earlier eras, white racists claimed that people of color feel injury less than whites. Until re-cently, many physicians alleged that human infants can't feel pain.

Whether out of ignorance or self-serving denial, fishers generally say the same of fishes.

Humans born with a rare condition called congenital analgesia can't feel pain. They repeatedly bite their tongue and lips; remain unaware of cuts, fractures, and infections, which go untended; and unknowingly apply weight to injured muscles and bones, causing further injury. They rarely live to age 40. Pain is protective. It tells people what to avoid. If nonhumans couldn't experience and remember pain, they continually would harm themselves.

In some ways, nonhumans apparently are *more* pain-sensitive than humans. For example, the nerve-endings in fish skin (which is extremely fragile) react to noxious pressure at a lower level than those in human skin. The fish nerve-endings have thresholds comparable to those of a human cornea.[16] When handled, a fish may feel as you would if someone were pressing on your cornea.

The scientific consensus is that all vertebrates can experience pain.[17] Substance P is a chemical associated with pain in humans. All vertebrates have substance P activity.

The human body also produces opiates, neurochemicals that reduce pain. For example, the body releases endorphins after injury, enabling escape action that otherwise would be too painful. All vertebrates have natural opiates.

Humans show less behavior indicative of pain when they receive opiate drugs, such as morphine. So do all other vertebrates. In experiments, rainbow trouts had acetic acid injected into their lips. They breathed more rapidly than normally, wouldn't eat for three hours, rocked from side to side, and rubbed their lips against their tank's walls and gravel floor.[18] Trouts react less to acetic acid if they're also injected with morphine.[19] Similarly, morphine reduces the reaction of rats, frogs, crocodiles, and other vertebrates to electric shock or a hot surface.[20]

Nonhumans act as if they feel pain. Many goat enslavers burn away kids' horn buds with a red-hot iron. As the iron is pressed to their head, the kids struggle and, often, scream. (Some die from shock—further evidence of severe pain.)[21] At slaughter, salmons are dumped into water infused with carbon dioxide. Before they become paralyzed, they make "vigorous attempts to escape."[22] Why would fishes try to escape from water? Carbon dioxide is painful to breathe.

On "fur farms," foxes are electrocuted. With one electrode in their anus and another inside their mouth or clipped to their lip, they remain conscious as the current passes through their body. They scream before dying of cardiac arrest.

Nonhuman vertebrates learn to avoid noxious stimuli. For example, toads who are stung by a honeybee subsequently avoid bees.[23] In thousands of experiments, pigeons, goldfishes, rats, and other vertebrates have learned to avoid electric shock. Why would nonhumans take preventive action unless they experience pain? How could they learn and remember if stings and shocks didn't involve conscious experience?

I strongly disapprove of pain experiments on nonhumans (as well as all other exploitive experimentation, invasive or not). Whenever I cite vivisection, I do so reluctantly, only to provide additional evidence that stubborn skeptics may find convincing. In my view, the wealth of evidence available from nonexploitive observation of nonhumans more than suffices to demonstrate their sentience, especially given the shared ancestry of all nervous systems.

The claim that only humans experience pain, or that all humans are more sensitive to pain than all nonhumans, has no scientific basis.

An old-speciesist might object, "Humans have more capacity to suffer because they can experience grief, fear, and other negative emotions." Other animals, too, feel such emotions. In fact, many nonhumans apparently feel more deeply than many humans.

While the male parakeet Blue Bird was in another room, the female parakeet Blondie—new to the household—was placed in his cage. When Blue Bird flew back to his cage and saw Blondie, he burst into excited calls and aerial acrobatics. Landing on the cage, he chirped to his new companion. The two soon became ardent lovers. They often sat cuddling and twittering. Blue Bird, who spoke and understood numerous English words and phrases, would lavish Blondie with endearments. "Pretty Blondie, give me a kiss," he would say. Then they would rub their beaks together or open them and kiss with intertwined tongues. Frequently Blue Bird sang to an enraptured Blondie or delighted her by flying in impressive zigzags. They made love face to face while Blue Bird embraced Blondie with one wing. After seven years with Blondie, Blue Bird died. Blondie became lethargic and unsociable. When a parakeet named Lover joined the household, Blondie rejected his company. They never became lovers or friends.[24] Blondie's suffering had nothing to do with physical pain. Her pain was psychological. She mourned.

Sometimes, forced to choose between physical and psychological suffering, nonhumans choose physical suffering, as when a dog enters a burning room to save a human child and suffers burns as a result. Why would a dog do this unless the psychological pain caused by the child's death would exceed the physical pain of burns?

The behavior of many nonhuman captives makes their mental suffering painfully clear. Throughout each pregnancy, a sow enslaved by the pig-flesh industry is isolated in a stall with iron bars and a concrete floor. The stall is so narrow that she has room only to stand up and lie down. If the stall is open in the rear, she also is chained to the floor by a neck collar or body harness. When first chained inside a pregnancy stall, a sow typically reacts with violent escape attempts lasting up to several hours. She screams, repeatedly yanks her chain, twists and thrashes, and crashes against the stall's bars before collapsing. After her futile struggle to break free, she lies motionless, groaning and whimpering, her snout reaching outward beneath the bars. Finally she sits for long periods with her head drooping and her eyes vacant or closed.[25]

Nonhumans often may suffer *more* intensely than humans in similar situations. Sometimes nonhumans manage to escape from human abuse. Usually, however, confinement and other physical coercion render escape impossible. Nonhuman victims of inescapable human abuse can't make sense of their plight, change their circumstances, or foresee an end to their suffering. Being able to understand or partially control one's fate makes adversity more bearable. Humans are good at rationalizing ("It's God's will," "My suffering will be rewarded"). What consoles the chained sow, the zoo-imprisoned orangutan, the caged and solitary parrot who never will fly? There's no reason to believe that other animals suffer less sharply or deeply than humans.

More Intelligence

Old-speciesists rank humans above nonhumans in intelligence. However, some nonhumans surpass some humans in the kind of intelligence typical of humans.

Humans pride themselves on possessing a large brain. On average, the Neanderthal brain was larger. Elephants and many cetaceans have bigger, heavier brains than ours, with more nerve cells. For their body weight, many small birds and mammals (e.g., canaries, house sparrows, and pygmy tree shrews) have heavier brains than humans. Further, the brains of many small vertebrates show greater neural density and interconnectedness. "Larger brains are not necessarily more efficient and more powerful than smaller brains," Harvard University neuroanatomist Terrence Deacon notes.[26]

Humans boast that their brain contains many anatomically and functionally distinct areas. However, differentiation generally increases with brain size. A smaller brain, Deacon explains, doesn't require as many distinct areas to process information with equal ease and speed. Human perception of an integrated visual image involves numerous brain areas specialized for detection of shape, brightness, movement, and other visual properties. A squirrel's brain registers and coordinates visual properties in only a few areas. Structural complexity doesn't automatically signify brain "advancement," Deacon cautions.[27]

In any case, some brain regions are organizationally *simpler* in humans than in other animals. As neuroanatomists note, the pretectum (involved in visuomotor behavior) is more "differentiated" and "elaborated" in birds, reptiles, and fishes than in humans.[28] Many fishes generate electric fields with which they detect objects and signal; their cerebellum is "far more complex" than ours.[29] Numerous nonhumans possess brain structures that humans entirely lack.

Even so, humans and all other vertebrates possess the same basic cerebral circuitry, with nerve-cell populations that correspond in their chemistry, connections, and apparent functions. Popularly regarded as lowly creatures, sharks exhibit cerebral "organization comparable to that of other vertebrates, including mammals."[30]

Nonhuman behavior continually refutes the assertion that only humans reason. While a family of beavers slept in their lodge, a vandal tore a large hole in their dam. Water escaped with such force that the beavers' pond soon would drain. Emerging from the family lodge at his usual time of early evening, the father beaver rapidly swam to the dam and, wide-eyed, observed its condition. Quickly he crossed the pond, felled a large shrub, dragged it into the water, towed it to the break, and wedged it into the top of the dam's wall. He repeated this process, which failed to stanch the outflow, only once. By sight and sound, the pond's water loss was obvious only at the surface, yet the beaver addressed underwater damage. He started to uproot lily plants (usually reserved for eating) and began using them to plug the dam's underwater leaks. Soon three of his offspring emerged from the lodge and hurried to assist him. The four beavers worked to repair the dam with vegetation, mud, and sticks. Whenever dissatisfied with his offspring's placement of sticks, the father repositioned them for greater tightness and stability. The beavers labored throughout the night. The next day while the beavers slept, human volunteers carried sticks to the dam. When the father beaver emerged from the lodge at his usual time, he pulled a log from the roof and towed it to the dam. Clearly, he remembered the urgent need for building materials. With cries of joy, he discovered the pile of sticks left by human well-wishers. He started putting the sticks to use. Soon four of his offspring arrived, towing logs that they too had removed from the lodge. Of those beavers able to help, only the mother stayed behind, to care for newborn kits. In addition to making the dam leak-proof, the beavers added six inches to its height, so that future rainfall would raise the pond's water level.[31] Beavers plan, deduce, and act accordingly.

Invariably, speciesists define intelligence in a way that favors humans. For example, they require evidence of abstract thinking. Experimentation has demonstrated that nonhumans form abstract concepts, including before/after, smaller/larger, same/different, number, analogy, and "none."[32]

Even if every nonhuman lacked the capacity for human-like reasoning, nonhumans wouldn't be inferior. Why equate typically human characteristics with superiority? Because *we* possess them? In the same self-aggrandizing and otherwise-arbitrary way, a superb singer could declare, "I can remember intricate melodies and sing them beautifully. The ability to do that signifies superiority." Then vocally gifted humans, many songbirds, and perhaps other nonhumans such as humpback whales would qualify for rights. Creatures with no singing ability, including most rock stars, would not.

Because human culture features verbal language, speciesists tend to equate verbal capacity with reasoning ability. Nonhumans have their own forms of communication, which we're just beginning to detect and decipher. Gunnison's prairie dogs vocalize in ways that identify other animals by group membership (e.g., as a human, dog, coyote, or hawk) but also as individuals.[33] Rodents such as rats, mice, hamsters, and gerbils communicate in ultrasound, too high-frequency for us to hear without technology. Larger nonhuman animals such as alligators, hippos, elephants, and fin whales vocalize in infrasound, too low-frequency for our unaided ears. Fishes of at least hundreds of species communicate with sounds ranging from buzzes and clicks to yelps and sobs. We can hear most such sounds only through hydrophones. Electric fishes "read" one another's discharges, which vary according to the signaler's age, species, individual identity, and intentions (e.g., courtship or rivalry).

Requiring human-like intelligence in nonhumans is comparable to requiring crow-like intelligence in humans. It's inherently biased. Humans wouldn't rank so high in intelligence if the criteria for superiority included an individual's ability to survive without assistance or without comforting myths. While calling themselves "the rational species," humans generally are quite irrational: bigoted, self-deceiving, self-destructive, passionate about trivia such as sports scores. Would intelligent beings riot over the outcome of a soccer game? Smoke, eat, and drink themselves to death? Poison the water, soil, and air on which they rely? Believe that other religions are false but *theirs* is true? Would they accord respect based on an individual's skin color, nationality, sex, or species?

Some humans have much higher IQs than others. Should the law permit those with high IQs to enslave or murder those with low IQs? We don't accord rights in proportion to a human's IQ. In the 2002 case *Atkins v. Virginia*, the U.S. Supreme Court ruled that capital punishment of humans with profound mental disabilities is unconstitutional. The law affords special protections to humans of exceptionally low mental capacity. Yet, the allegedly lower intelligence of nonhumans is cited as justification for denying them rights.

Those who disqualify nonhumans from rights on the grounds that they lack human-like intelligence unwittingly disqualify many humans as well. Humans differ widely in their cognitive abilities, which overlap with nonhuman ones. If no nonhuman can solve complex equations or write a philosophical treatise, neither can most humans. Even by conventional standards, a mature catfish is in many ways more cognizant than a newborn or senile human, and the average pigeon or rat possesses greater learning and reasoning ability than many humans with mental disabilities.

According to tests designed for humans, the gorilla Koko has an IQ of about 90, close to the human average.[34] In 1982 the U.S. Supreme Court affirmed the rights of Nicholas Romeo, a 33-year-old man with an IQ one-tenth of Koko's: about 9. Believed to possess the mental capacity of an average 18-month-old infant, this man showed no language ability.[35] In contrast, Koko understands spoken English and communicates in American Sign Language using a vocabulary of more than a thousand words.[36]

Someone might argue, "Even if some humans are no smarter than some nonhumans, we should err on the side of caution and protect all humans." Then, why not consistently err on the side of caution and protect all nonhumans as well?

Normal human intelligence isn't a valid criterion for basic rights. Any signs of thought indicate that an individual is conscious, capable of experiencing. Beyond that, intelligence is morally irrelevant. Regardless of their degree of human-like intelligence, nonhumans would greatly benefit from laws protecting them from human harm.

We don't require that a human possess any particular level of intelligence in order to have rights. Democratic societies protect all human animals, whatever their intellectual capacity. The same should apply to other animals.

Superior Morality

Of all supposed reasons for denying rights to nonhumans, the most hypocritical is the claim that humans are morally superior. People who argue that only humans are sufficiently moral to deserve rights demonstrate their own immorality. They selfishly seek to keep speciesist abuse legal.

According to the *American Heritage Dictionary*, "brutal" traits such as "unfeeling cruelty" are "more characteristic of lower animals than of human beings." But the usage example cites *human* behavior: "brutal" bull-baiting and cockfighting.[37] The example reveals the ironic truth: humans are the "brutes"; nonhumans are their victims.

Overwhelmingly, it's humans who needlessly hurt and kill. Nonhuman predators aren't cruel; they kill to survive. Sport hunters and fishers wound and kill for fun. It's rare for nonhuman predators to unnecessarily prolong killing. From vivisectors to bull-"fighters," many humans routinely torture nonhumans to death. Each day, flesh purveyors kill millions of fishes, birds, mammals, and other animals for profit. For mere convenience and taste, consumers eat the remains. Every moment, millions of nonhumans enslaved by humans live in cruel confinement. How many humans feel anger, sorrow, or pain for the caged hen, the whale confined to a tank, the elephant in chains? Humans have no rivals in "unfeeling cruelty."

Many humans routinely abuse other humans as well. Child abuse, spouse abuse, and other forms of intra-human violence are widespread. Who's more moral: the rapist who leaves his victim to die or the dog who fetches help for the victim? Many nonhumans evince more goodness than many humans.

Consider Ginny, a small mixed-breed dog who was one year old when "shelter" workers found her dehydrated and starving. Evicted from their apartment, Ginny's owners had left her to die. Soon after her rescue and adoption, Ginny started rescuing others. On walks with her adopter, Philip Gonzalez, Ginny strained at her leash whenever she saw a homeless cat. One night, Gonzalez lost hold of her leash. Ginny ran into a vacant lot and up to a starving kitten, whom she licked and groomed. When she and Gonzalez arrived home, Ginny cried and scratched at the door until they set out again, with food. They returned to the kitten, who gobbled up their offering. From then on, Gonzalez regularly fed the kitten and other cats in the vacant lot. Barking loudly, Ginny once pulled Gonzalez toward a group of humans who were kicking a homeless cat. Gonzalez snatched the cat, took her for veterinary treatment, and brought her home. At first the cat cowered. Ginny provided reassurance. Quietly she stayed by the cat. When the cat permitted, Ginny bathed her in licks. The cat soon lost her fear. Throughout the years, Ginny has helped many cats. She readily detects feline injury, illness, disability, or fear and actively seeks to rescue or comfort cats in need. After Ginny whimpered and clambered at one kitten's "shelter" cage, Gonzalez adopted the kitten and discovered her to be deaf. Ginny shows great sensitivity toward this cat. She never barks at her or startles her by approaching from behind. Instead, circling around to the cat's front, Ginny moves within plain view. As stated by Gonzalez, "compassion" guides Ginny's life.[38]

You might be thinking, "Nonhumans aren't *self-consciously* kind.

Unlike humans, they don't contemplate moral alternatives and choose to do the right thing." We can't know the degree to which Ginny and other nonhumans are self-consciously moral, but there's strong evidence that nonhumans do make choices based on morality.

In experiments by psychologist Stanley Milgram, human subjects were told to give a man an electric shock every time that he answered a question incorrectly. Subjects faced no penalty if they refused to comply. Nevertheless, the majority pressed switches signaling increasingly powerful shocks, even after the man had started to plead and scream. Unknown to the subjects, the electric shocks were fake.[39]

In similar experiments using rhesus monkeys, the shocks were real. Monkeys learned to pull two chains for food. Then one of the chains was linked to a shock generator. Now, in addition to releasing food, this chain would inflict an electric shock on another monkey, visible in an adjoining cage. To get adequate food, a monkey needed to pull both chains. Unlike Milgram's subjects, the monkeys were forced to choose between equally grave alternatives: shock another monkey, or go hungry. Most monkeys went hungry. Apparently unwilling to risk giving even a single shock, two stopped pulling either chain and went completely without food—one for five days, the other for twelve.[40]

In the human experiments, most subjects believed that they were inflicting pain on a man guilty of nothing worse than incorrect answers. In the monkey experiments, humans robbed innocent beings of their freedom, deprived them of food, and subjected them to electric shocks. In contrast, most of the monkeys showed altruism, at considerable expense to themselves. *Who's* consciously moral?

Even if no nonhuman were capable of self-conscious morality, what difference would that make? Many humans—infants, sociopaths, adults with severe mental disabilities—aren't capable of self-conscious morality. That doesn't entitle us to deprive them of basic rights.

As philosopher Steve Sapontzis has pointed out, nonhumans often take actions that would be considered moral if taken by humans. We credit humans with goodness when they respond to others' needs with kindness and generosity, whether or not their virtue seems self-conscious. In fact, we tend to regard humans as *less* good to the extent that they're motivated by a sense of duty or self-righteousness rather than a desire to help others.[41]

In general, nonhumans are far more innocent than humans. Most nonhumans don't seriously injure or kill except out of immediate and direct survival need, as when a lion kills prey. They're innocent of serious wrongdoing. In contrast, most humans routinely participate in the needless infliction of suffering and death on nonhumans. While boasting of "human kindness," humans treat other animals with extreme injustice and cruelty. To someone who has shed speciesism's double standard, vivisection and food-industry captivity constitute false imprisonment and, in most cases, torture; trapping, slaughter, and commercial fishing are murder; and buying the resulting products (primarily flesh, skin, and hair) is being an accessory to murder. In proportion to their numbers, humans commit incomparably more guilty deeds (acts of intentional, needless harm) than nonhumans.

In psychological terms as well, nonhumans are more innocent. When they do cause needless harm, they might not recognize the harm as needless or harmful. In any case, we should give them the benefit of the doubt. In democratic societies, humans who might not know right from wrong aren't held accountable for injuring or killing others. They're presumed innocent unless compelling evidence indicates otherwise. A democratic society deprives humans of freedom only when conscious guilt can be demonstrated beyond a reasonable doubt. By the legal standards of democratic nations, nonhumans are innocent.

Except for very young children and adults with severe mental disabilities, humans who eat a "hamburger" understand that it's a product of slaughter. Also, many flesh-eating humans know that they needn't eat flesh. Most humans certainly understand that they needn't visit zoos, wear nonhuman skin or hair, or support the breeding of nonhumans as pets. Yet, these practices continue on a massive scale, along with numerous other speciesist practices. Indeed, many humans participate in nonhuman exploitation even though, by their own admission, they consider that exploitation immoral. For example, they continue to eat flesh and other animal-derived foods after they've concluded that doing so is wrong.

In some sense, of course, many (perhaps most) humans *don't* know right from wrong. Society has told them that it's acceptable to harm other animals, and they've internalized that belief. Still, with regard to human victims, the law doesn't accept the victimizer's enculturation as justification. Defense lawyers don't plead that their clients should be excused for violence against women or people of color on the grounds that those clients have been brought up in a sexist, racist society. Misogyny doesn't exonerate a rapist. Racism doesn't exonerate a white who kills a black. To the contrary, acts of violence often receive harsher penalties if they're judged to be expressions of bigotry: hate crimes. Therefore, unless we apply a double standard, speciesist acts are unjust. Morally, their perpetrators are as guilty as perpetrators of crimes that entail other forms of prejudice.

Overwhelmingly, nonhumans are innocent and humans are guilty, whether we assess innocence and guilt in terms of an individual's actions, understanding, or both. Humans morally superior to other animals? If only that were true.

Old-speciesists offer no valid justification for limiting moral and legal rights to humans. Some merely express a preference for members of their own species. Others cite the Bible. Still others fail to see nonhumans as individuals. Many point to characteristics, such as reasoning ability and morality, supposedly unique to humans. In reality, each of these characteristics is more abundant in some nonhumans than in some humans. Most importantly, sentience is the only logical criterion for basic rights.

Old speciesism is entirely untenable. Yet, as you'll see in the next chapter, current law is entirely old-speciesist.

3

Old-Speciesist Law

Current law treats nonhumans and humans in drastically different ways. It affords individual nonhumans no meaningful protection. In the United States, as elsewhere, humans are the only animals who have legal rights. Under the law, humans are "persons" whereas nonhumans are "animals." "Persons" have legal rights; "animals" don't.

Property

Legally, "animals" are human property. In the United States a free-living deer, bass, or blue jay is public property. A cow commercially exploited for her milk is personal property. So is a cat or dog living with a human family.

Some cruelty statutes appear under the heading "Crimes against Property" or "Property Destruction and Defacement." When a Virginia woman took a neglected, roaming cat to a veterinarian for medical treatment and "spaying," the cat's owners complained to the authorities. The state charged the good Samaritan with "defacing or injury of personal property." (She was acquitted.)[1]

Killing a nonhuman owned by someone else brings a charge of theft, not murder. As legal scholar and animal rights theorist Gary Francione has explained, instead of protecting nonhumans, the law protects human property interests *in* nonhumans.[2]

Although a bulldog was having trouble breathing, a veterinarian placed her on her back for artificial insemination. The bulldog started to struggle. When her owner tried to restrain her, the bulldog bit the owner on the hand. The owner immediately was taken to the hospital. In her absence the forced insemination continued. The bulldog's breathing worsened. Still the forced insemination continued. Struggling to breathe, the bulldog died. A veterinary newsletter reported these events as a case of potential liability: the bulldog's owner could sue the vet for injury (the bite wound) and loss of property (the bulldog).[3] From a nonspeciesist perspective, both the vet and the bulldog's owner should have been charged with felonies: sexual assault and murder of the bulldog.

U.S. criminal codes define murder as unjustifiably killing an "individual" or "person." A dog is an individual. But the law defines *individual* as a human individual. It also restricts "persons" to humans (individual humans as well as entities, such as corporations and governmental bodies, that represent some group of humans).

Usually, injuring or killing a nonhuman is a crime only if it qualifies as damaging or destroying someone else's property. A number of states exonerate people from injuring or killing nonhumans if the perpetrators own the victims or act with an owner's permission. As expressed by Tennessee law, the owner of a nonhuman animal has a "right to the animal's life."[4] Nonhumans have no legal right to their *own* lives.

Under U.S. law, guardians (often court-appointed) protect the legal rights of mentally incompetent humans, such as children and the senile. Denied legal rights, nonhumans have no such guardians.

Humans seeking legal redress for wrongs committed against nonhumans must sue on their *own* behalf; to prevail, they must demonstrate that *they* have been harmed. If a human abuses a nonhuman owned by someone else, the human owner—not the nonhuman victim—is "the aggrieved party."

Overall, the law treats nonhumans as replaceable. Their worth is their market value, as if they were a camera or wristwatch. Some laws value nonhumans *less* than inanimate property: to protect such property, a human may legally kill a nonhuman.

Increasingly, courts are treating humans' nonhuman companions as a special class of personal property. In a 1979 New York City case, a woman sued a veterinarian who sent her a cat's remains rather than the body of her euthanized poodle companion. Ordinarily, New York State law doesn't allow damages for emotional distress resulting from loss of personal property. The judge, however, awarded such damages. "A pet is not just a thing but occupies a special place somewhere in between a person and a piece of personal property," he stated.[5] Similarly, in a 1994 Texas case a hunter who fatally shot two dogs was ordered to pay their owners thousands of dollars. "Animals are not *merely* property," one of the judges commented. As "sentient and emotive beings," they belong to "a unique category of 'property.'"[6] In such cases, however, the judgments simply increase the financial damages that the plaintiff(s) can receive. The judges recognize the importance of nonhuman companions *to their owners*. They treat the nonhumans who died as a special class of property, but still property.

In a 2001 Wisconsin Supreme Court case, a woman sought damages for emotional distress caused by the killing of her canine companion, whom a police officer shot. The court denied damages but remarked that a "companion dog" differs from inanimate property in having a "relationship" with, and special value to, a human.[7] The court did *not* suggest that dogs have rights or inherent value. The chief justice correctly noted, "This case is about the rights of a pet owner," not "about animal rights."[8]

"Wildlife Conservation" Laws

The Marine Mammal Protection Act (MMPA), the Endangered Species Act (ESA), and other "wildlife conservation" laws are old-speciesist. They afford some protection to species and other groups but accord no rights to individual nonhumans.

The MMPA is designed to protect "species and population stocks," not individuals.[9] It expresses "concern for the health and safety of dolphin populations," not dolphin individuals.[10] Like fishers, hunters, and trappers, the MMPA refers to nonhuman individuals as if they were species: kill "any species of whale" ("a whale of any species" would be correct).[11] The MMPA's framers weren't thinking in terms of nonhuman individuals even when referring to the killing of individual whales.

The MMPA doesn't forbid injuring and killing; it sets limits on injuring and killing. For example, it maintains a quota on tuna fishers' collateral killing of dolphins.[12] According to the MMPA, the government may allow the intentional killing of individual seals who eat salmons (whom humans want to eat).[13]

The MMPA's goal is to keep marine mammal populations at levels conducive to maximum human exploitation. For instance, the MMPA limits the killing of North Pacific fur seals to the extent necessary to keep herds "at their optimum sustainable population"—optimal for humans.[14] The MMPA also allows U.S. sport hunters to kill polar bears in Canada and import their body parts as trophies, provided that Canada maintains hunting quotas designed to keep the "affected population stock at a sustainable level."[15]

Imagine a human law equivalent to the MMPA—say, the Native American Protection Act. Because Native Americans constitute a small minority, they would be protected at the level of their various group populations. However, a certain number of individual Native Americans could be killed with impunity. The government would be concerned about the health and safety of Navajo, Onondaga, and other Native American populations, not individual Native Americans. The goal would be to keep group populations at "optimum sustainable" levels—optimal for *other* Americans. The government could allow the intentional killing of individual Chinooks who catch and eat salmons (whom other Americans want to catch and eat). Also, U.S. citizens could sport-hunt Inuits in Canada and import their body parts as trophies. In the 18th century, European-Americans did sport-hunt Native Americans and display their body parts.[16]

Like the MMPA, the ESA is aimed at preserving nonhuman groups. It too refers to the possession, sale, transport, and killing of "species," not individuals. The ESA promotes the "conservation" of "depleted" species, because of their "esthetic, ecological, educational, historical, recreational, and scientific value" to U.S. citizens, not because nonhumans have any rights or value of their own.[17]

Imagine a comparable Endangered Ethnicity Act (EEA). The act would be aimed at "conserving" low-population ethnic groups, such as Bedouins and Jews, because of their esthetic, ecological, educational, historical, recreational, and scientific value to other humans. The EEA would specify how many Bedouins and Jews could be killed and under what circumstances. Members of highly populous ethnic groups, such as the Chinese, could be killed in any number (until their population became small).

If we applied the ESA's principles to humans as a species, it would be legal to kill any number of humans until the human population was greatly reduced. Individual humans would have no rights.

Without laws like the MMPA and ESA, how would we protect species from extinction? By protecting every member of those species—that is, by according rights to nonhuman individuals. As ethicist Bernard Rollin has commented, "A species is a collection of morally relevant individuals."[18] Protect the individuals, and you've protected the species.

Cruelty Statutes

The 13th Amendment to the U.S. Constitution states, "Neither slavery nor involuntary servitude, except as a punishment for crime whereof the party shall have been duly convicted, shall exist within the United States." Nonhumans have committed no crime, yet they're enslaved: held as property. They're also subjected to involuntary servitude. Horses pull carriages. Camels trudge around zoo paddocks, with children on their backs. Capuchin monkeys serve as house slaves for quadriplegics, at whose bidding they perform menial tasks. Rather than prohibiting nonhuman enslavement, state cruelty statutes endorse and perpetuate it, along with its worst abuses.

Although loading, riding, or working nonhumans constitutes involuntary servitude, states prohibit only overloading, overriding, and overworking. How much riding or working is too much? Pennsylvania specifies: more than 15 hours a day or 90 hours a week (more than double a fulltime human work load).[19] In some states, even overworking a nonhuman isn't punishable unless the nonhuman was "seriously" or "grossly" overworked.[20]

Because nonhumans legally are objects of use, cruelty statutes exempt even the cruelest speciesist exploitation from prosecution. As Francione shows in *Animals, Property, and the Law*, cruelty is legal if it's business as usual.[21] By various means, cruelty statutes leave the most common forms of cruelty untouched.

Some states exclude the most frequently abused animals from cruelty coverage. Iowa's general cruelty statute excludes all invertebrates; free-living fishes, reptiles, amphibians, "furbearers," "game" birds, and "game" mammals; "poultry"; and "livestock."[22] Instead of protecting nonhumans, the statute protects fishing, trapping, hunting, and "animal agriculture."

With regard to pigs, Iowa is a major slave state. In the preceding chapter, you read how sows are restrained during pregnancy. The crate in which a sow gives birth and nurses her piglets is even more confining than the pregnancy stall. Metal bars directly above the sow restrict her to a lying position, or straps bind her to the floor. Sows and boars are fed only once every two or three days (just enough to leave them able to reproduce), so they're perpetually hungry. Soon after birth, piglets have their ears notched, needle teeth clipped, and tail cut off—all without anesthetic. As previously mentioned, male piglets also are castrated without anesthetic. Prematurely taken from their mother, piglets are confined to cages stacked in rows. Each cage commonly imprisons eight to ten piglets. Forced to stand on wire mesh, each piglet has less than two square feet of floor space. At about two months of age, the pigs are crowded into pens with concrete, slatted floors. By the time they go to slaughter, many pigs are crippled. Most have pneumonia, from breathing ammonia produced by accumulated waste. Is it any wonder that Iowa excludes pigs from its general cruelty statute?

The Eighth Amendment to the Constitution prohibits "cruel and unusual punishment" of human prisoners convicted of a crime. In the case of such prisoners, the Supreme Court has ruled all of the following to be unlawfully cruel: crowding prisoners; depriving them of exercise; torturing them; and failing to provide them with adequate food and water, needed medical care, or a sanitary, ventilated environment.[23] Pigs suffer all of these abuses, which are cruel but usual. And pigs have committed no crime. They shouldn't be imprisoned in the first place. No human needs to eat pig flesh. Imprisoning pigs is wholly unnecessary and unjust.

Many cruelty statutes expressly exempt the most common forms of speciesist abuse, such as rodeo, horse racing, zoos, aquaprisons, vivisection, and "animal agriculture." About half exempt trapping; about half, sport fishing. Although courts never have interpreted cruelty statutes as prohibiting hunting, most cruelty statutes expressly exempt hunting.

A brain shot that kills instantly is rare in gun hunting and virtually nonexistent in bowhunting. Most hunters of large mammals don't aim for the head, but the heart–lung area. Unconsciousness and death are rapid (but not immediate) only if a gunshot or arrow ruptures the heart or aorta. An animal shot anywhere other than the brain, heart, or a major blood vessel experiences prolonged suffer-

ing. An animal gun-shot in the lungs suffers intense pain and suffocates when the lungs collapse or fill with blood. After an arrow shot
to the heart–lung area, bowhunters generally wait at least half an
hour before tracking, to allow time for the wounded animal to die
from blood loss. A belly shot causes extreme pain. After a belly shot,
bowhunters wait eight to twelve hours before tracking—again, to allow time for the wounded animal to die. Animals who escape with
lesser arrow wounds commonly die, over days or weeks, from painful bacterial infection.

Except under the rarest circumstances, no human must hunt in
order to survive in good health. Yet, each year, U.S. hunters kill
more than 125 million nonhumans, excluding untold millions killed
illegally or left fatally wounded.[24] Under the U.S. Code, killing
someone by "lying in wait" (hiding, watching, and waiting) is first-
degree murder—if the victim is human. Hunters lie in wait.

Humans certainly wouldn't call hunting a sport if they were the
ones being wounded and killed. According to one hunter, any hunter
who accidentally shoots another human should be imprisoned for
causing suffering or death and showing a "flagrant," "callous" disregard for life.[25] Suffering and death are no less real when they befall
nonhumans. Doesn't killing for sport show the *most* flagrant disregard for life? Isn't it more callous to kill intentionally than to kill accidentally?

Society shares hunters' disregard of nonhumans by including
only humans within the phrase *hunting fatalities*. Most hunting fatalities are, of course, nonhuman. To any nonspeciesist, hunting that
fails to kill is attempted murder, and successful hunting is first-
degree murder.

As previously mentioned, in former times some European-
Americans hunted Native Americans for sport. Today we find such
"sport" grotesquely immoral. Sport hunting of nonhumans is equally
immoral.

Many cruelty statutes exempt all "accepted" practices within an
area of speciesist abuse. Accepted by whom? The abusers themselves. For example, Maine allows "normally accepted husbandry
practices" that *fail* to provide food-industry captives with "adequate
freedom of movement" and "humanely clean" conditions.[26]

In the United States, chickens and turkeys reared for slaughter
live amid tens of thousands crowded across a floor. Throughout their

confinement, the litter accumulates excrement. As the litter becomes wet, hard, and ammonia-saturated, the birds develop foot ulcers, ankle burns, breast blisters and ulcers, and respiratory and eye disease, including blindness. By slaughter time, each turkey has only about three square feet of space; each chicken has less than one square foot.

More than 99 percent of U.S. hens exploited for their eggs spend their lives confined to wire cages. From a pit below, mounds of excrement saturate the air with eye-stinging ammonia. On average, each cage holds eight hens. The hens are squeezed side to side on a sloping wire floor. They're crammed in too tightly to lift a wing or even stand comfortably. The cages are filthy with feathers and excrement. Many hens become caught in the cage wire and die unable to reach food or water. Because caged "laying hens" get no exercise and constant egg production robs their bones of calcium, they suffer from severe osteoporosis. Many lose the ability to stand or even sit upright. By the time they're killed, most have broken bones.

The Supreme Court has ruled that crowding four or more human prisoners into a cell of 80 square feet is "cruel and unusual punishment" and therefore illegal.[27] Compare 20 square feet per human with a turkey's three square feet, a "broiler chicken's" one square foot, or a "laying hen's" standard six by eight *inches*.

If Maine's cruelty statute outlawed failure to provide chickens and turkeys with "adequate freedom of movement" and "humanely clean" conditions, it would, in effect, outlaw most of the state's "poultry" industry. Chickens and turkeys, like pigs, have committed no crime. They shouldn't be imprisoned at all.

Because speciesist exploitation is inherently abusive, some cruelty statutes essentially say, "Oh, do whatever you want if it's standard." South Dakota allows "mistreatment, torture, cruelty, neglect, abandonment, mutilation, or inhumane slaughter of an animal . . . consistent with generally accepted training, use, and husbandry procedures."[28] Isn't the point of a cruelty statute to *prohibit* mistreatment, torture, and cruelty? No. As Francione emphasizes, the point is to prohibit *aberrant* mistreatment, torture, and cruelty—mistreatment that isn't a customary part of speciesist exploitation.[29]

Nonhumans most need protection against the most prevalent forms of cruelty, but such protection would outlaw institutionalized speciesism. Overwhelmingly, cruelty statutes sanction, rather than prohibit, cruelty.

In addition to allowing the most common forms of speciesist exploitation, cruelty statutes allow the killing of nonhumans who are considered a nuisance. Some cruelty statutes expressly exempt "pest control." Although sanitation remains the most effective means of reducing rat and mouse reproduction, "pest control" employs cruelty. Anticoagulant poisons cause rats and mice to die, over days, from internal bleeding. The poison bromethalin causes painful fluid retention in the brain and spinal cord; death can take several days or longer. Licensed fumigators use carbon dioxide or sulfuryl fluoride. Carbon dioxide kills by suffocation and is painful to breathe at lower concentrations. Sulfuryl fluoride causes seizures and fluid in the lungs. Rats and mice also are killed with spring and glue traps. Spring traps break their back. Glue traps grip their limbs. The rat or mouse slowly suffocates from the glue, dies of starvation and dehydration, or—tossed alive into the trash—is otherwise killed by the process of waste disposal. If it's acceptable to kill rats and mice because their high numbers can cause inconvenience or contribute to disease, why isn't it acceptable to kill humans for the same reasons?

Do cruelty statutes protect *any* nonhumans? Primarily they protect dogs, cats, horses, and other mammals kept as pets—but only minimally. First, most cruelty to pets is committed in the privacy of people's homes, so it never becomes public. Second, most cases of known cruelty aren't prosecuted. Third, due to all the caveats regarding cruel acts (such as the requirement of intent to harm), it's hard to win cruelty convictions. Fourth, convictions usually bring paltry penalties. Imprisonment for a cruelty offense is rare. A New Jersey couple failed to feed dozens of dogs, cats, and other nonhumans. Some starved to death. The authorities found the others emaciated. Many of the victims were lying in their own waste. The couple received no jail time, only fines.[30]

Perhaps most importantly, cruelty statutes don't prohibit humans from breeding other animals. Humans have no moral right to breed nonhumans—ever. Breeding is enslavement's point of origin. (Before black emancipation, U.S. slaveholders exercised considerable control over the breeding of their human captives. Slaveholders applied terms such as *breeder*, *stock*, and *selective breeding* to both their nonhuman and human property.) Without human manipulation of nonhuman breeding, abusive industries such as vivisection and "animal agriculture" would be impractical.

Any attempt to perpetuate a particular trait in nonhumans involves restricting the gene pool. So-called selective breeding largely is inbreeding. Because the mated animals are so similar genetically, selective breeding commonly pairs harmful recessive genes. Disabilities result. Many hatchery-born trouts have deformed lips, jaws, and gill plates. Severely inbred, captive-born cheetahs easily succumb to infectious disease and rarely have healthy offspring. Captive minks are prone to deafness, immune deficiency, twisted necks, bleeding membranes, and painful uterine contractions. The majority of "purebred" dogs suffer from some unintended inherited disability. Dalmatians are prone to deafness, poodles to epilepsy, and boxers to malignant tumors. Congenital heart disease afflicts "purebred" dogs at more than triple the rate in mixed breeds.[31] On average, each breed of "purebred" dogs harbors over a dozen genetic defects.[32]

In many cases, humans have intentionally bred disabilities into nonhumans. Some hatcheries have bred trouts to be light-sensitive albinos, whom sport fishers spot more easily. The bird-flesh industry has bred chickens and turkeys to grow far more rapidly than is natural and be top-heavy with breast flesh. The birds' skeletons haven't kept pace. Because their legs can't support their weight, most chickens and turkeys have difficulty walking or even standing. The sheep-hair industry has bred merino sheep to have excessively wrinkled skin (which results in more "wool"). The skin-folds collect moisture and attract flies, who lay eggs that hatch into flesh-eating larvae. Excessive hair makes merino sheep susceptible to fatal overheating. Numerous canine health problems directly relate to a "purebred's" prescribed look. Dogs have been bred to be oversized, undersized, narrow-faced, and flat-faced. Short-limbed dogs such as dachshunds and basset hounds are afflicted with dwarfism that often leads to lameness, paralysis, or excruciating compression of the spinal cord. Cats, too, have been bred to have pathologies that humans find cute or fashionable. Persians and Himalayans are flat-faced; sphinxes are hairless; munchkins have short limbs. Twisty cats have short, nonfunctional front legs, which force them to hop like kangaroos.

Morally there's no such thing as a "responsible breeder." A vast amount of cruelty begins with breeding.

As Francione has stated, cruelty statutes apply to a "relatively minuscule" amount of cruelty and don't provide nonhumans with "any meaningful level of protection."[33] Cruelty statutes deal almost exclusively with sadism or anomalous, egregious neglect—because such abuse doesn't further the use of nonhumans as property.[34]

Humans legally can do virtually anything to their nonhuman property, provided that they're engaged in some traditional form of speciesist abuse, such as vivisection, hunting, or "animal agriculture." If public bull torture were traditional in the United States, as it is in Spain, it would be legal in the United States. A U.S. resident who beats a dog to death may easily face prosecution because beating a dog to death isn't standard practice in any traditional speciesist activity. However, a U.S. resident who tortures a dog to death in laboratory experimentation is exempt from prosecution—thanks, in part, to the Animal Welfare Act.

Animal Welfare Act

Like state cruelty statutes, the U.S. Animal Welfare Act (AWA) protects the exploitation of nonhumans far more than it protects nonhumans. The Act doesn't cover most nonhumans subjected to cruelty, even within the areas of speciesist abuse that it addresses: the pet trade, nonhuman exhibition (aquaprisons, zoos, circuses, and other "animal acts"), and vivisection. Invertebrates, amphibians, fishes, reptiles, and many mammals and birds are excluded from coverage.

In warehouses holding hundreds of thousands of parakeets, canaries, or other birds, pairs kept as breeders for the pet trade are confined for life in a small cage with only food, water, and a nest box. Birds bred for sale usually are too young to feed themselves when they're sold to pet stores. Often, instead of receiving the multiple daily feedings that they need, they go hungry or even starve to death. Routinely, pet stores kill sick birds by placing them in a freezer. To date, no AWA regulations pertain to birds. As a result of a 2002 amendment to the AWA, regulations are planned regarding birds in the pet trade. Will these regulations significantly change the pet industry's treatment of birds? That's highly unlikely. AWA regulations have failed to protect other animals exploited by the pet industry.

AWA regulations addressing pet-industry exploitation of dogs have existed for decades. U.S. puppy mills annually breed over half a million "purebred" dogs for sale in pet stores. Females kept for breeding are bred every ovulation cycle and killed at age five or six, when their "production" declines. Most spend their entire life alone in a small, dirty wire cage—denied all exercise. Usually the cages are outside, so the dogs are exposed to every weather extreme. Often they receive inadequate food and water, which may freeze in its bowl. On some puppy mills, dogs are debarked: their vocal cords are severed. Dogs in puppy mills commonly have filthy, matted hair; rotted teeth; and untreated wounds. They suffer from a list of ailments, including foot abscesses, ear infections, severe mange, oozing and ulcerated eyes, and heartworm. Many hobble because they injured or severed a limb in their cage's wire floor. Puppies from puppy mills—the vast majority of those sold in pet stores—are prone to health problems caused by inbreeding and deplorable treatment.

So much for the AWA with regard to the pet trade. What about "animal" exhibition?

Aquaprisons legally can, and do, use tanks in which sea turtles barely have room to swim, alligators are too cramped to move more than one body length in any direction, electric eels have scarcely enough room to straighten out, and octopuses can't fully extend their tentacles. Fishes in aquaprisons find the conditions so adverse that they rarely survive longer than a few months.

In zoos most reptiles, amphibians, and invertebrates are confined behind glass and never go outside. Many zoo-imprisoned birds never fly, feel fresh air, or see the sky.

Mistreatment of "performing animals" often extends to battery. In alligator shows, humans sit, stand, and jump on alligators; drag them by their tail; "wrestle" them; hit and poke them on the nose, in the nostrils, and in the eyes; and, having taped their jaws shut, toss them into the air and pass them around to audience members.

Again, the AWA covers only some mammals and birds, and regulations pertaining to birds don't exist yet.

Most mammals in aquaprisons, zoos, and circuses are covered by the AWA. The Act's regulations allow these animals to be permanently confined with enough space only for "postural adjustments" such as standing up, lying down, and turning around.[35]

Aquaprison-confined dolphins and orcas are kept in small, barren tanks. Most die prematurely from stress-related infection.

In U.S. zoos, small mammals often are permanently confined

behind glass. Larger ones usually are confined indoors every night and throughout wintry weather. Typically they spend 16 hours a day in small, bare cells. Most elephants are kept chained at night; many are chained 16–17 hours a day. Most polar bears are confined to an enclosure one-millionth the size of their minimum natural range.[36] Yes, you read that correctly: one-millionth.

When they aren't performing, most mammals used in circuses are caged or chained. Circus cages generally provide barely enough room to turn around. Circuses frequently force elephants to perform when they're suffering from foot fissures, emaciation, or advanced tuberculosis.[37] Many elephants in circuses are arthritic and lame; most die prematurely.

As with animals not covered by the AWA, abuse of exhibited mammals often includes battery, especially of elephants. In zoos and circuses, elephants routinely are jabbed with a sharp hook, which easily draws blood, to make them move or obey commands. They're commonly "punished" with whippings, prolonged solitary confinement, food and water deprivation, repeated electric shocks, and beatings (with ax handles, baseball bats, and metal rods). Often they're tied down—splayed—and left that way for days, during which they're repeatedly beaten.[38]

So much for the AWA with regard to exhibition. That leaves vivisection.

The vast majority of mammals used in vivisection are excluded from AWA coverage: "rats of the genus *Rattus*, and mice of the genus *Mus*, bred for use in research."[39] By its own admission, the government has excluded these animals *because* so many of them are used in vivisection.[40] You've seen this strategy before, in cruelty statutes' exclusion of the very animals who are most often abused.

What can vivisectors legally do to mice and rats bred for vivisection? Virtually anything. Most mice and rats used in vivisection spend their lives in small, bare cages or shoebox-size plastic containers. Vivisectors breed mice to have all sorts of disabilities: severe immunodeficiency, cells that swell with waste material, convulsions, cancer. They inject mice with bacteria so that they lose limb function, bleed internally, and die of gangrene. They restrict mice, for hours at a time, to tubes in which they have room only to tremble. They give mice electric shocks, including in their corneas. Vivisectors dose rats with carcinogens, so that they become riddled with cancer in their bone marrow, lungs, and other organs. They burn rats with a flame, destroying every layer of skin over much of their body. They keep rats perpetually hungry or thirsty, so that they'll perform experimental tasks for food or water. They force rats to stay awake for weeks, until they nearly die. In a recent experiment, vivisectors subjected rats to three weeks of different forms of torture, including 24 hours without water, 40 hours without food, a forced swim in near-freezing water, five minutes in an oven at 104°F, two hours of immobilization in a tube 1½ inches in diameter, and, over a 35-minute period, 210 powerful foot-shocks.[41]

Vivisectors also can do virtually anything to other animals not covered by AWA regulations: invertebrates, amphibians, reptiles, fishes, "farm" mammals used in "agricultural" research, and birds. (Planned bird-use regulations won't apply to most bird vivisection: the AWA denies coverage to birds bred for "agriculture" or research.)

What can vivisectors do to animals *covered* by the AWA? Virtually anything. The AWA pledges noninterference with experimental design and procedure. Vivisectors can conduct any experiment in any manner they choose. For example, they often withhold anesthesia during painful procedures because it might interfere with results.

Monkeys have AWA coverage. Nevertheless, vivisectors do all of the following and more: cage them alone; give them electric shocks; dose them with nerve gas; deprive them of water 23 hours a day; slit open their skull, throat, chest, or abdomen and implant electrodes; fuse their upper neck vertebrae to their skull to limit head movement; immobilize them in a chair for weeks at a time; confine them, for months, to a narrow, high-walled chamber; and keep them totally isolated for the first six months of their lives.

The AWA is a sham. It legitimizes the breeding, sale, purchase, imprisonment, torture, and murder of nonhuman beings.

Quite apart from the fact that millions of dogs, cats, and other "domesticated" nonhumans currently need homes, no one needs to breed, sell, or buy nonhumans as pets. The pet trade shouldn't exist.

Nor does anyone need to exhibit nonhumans. Entertainment and supposed education don't justify imprisoning innocent individuals. For several weeks in 1906, the Bronx Zoo displayed the African "Pygmy" Ota Benga caged with the orangutan Dohong. After several weeks of protests, largely from African-Americans, the zoo stopped displaying Ota Benga. Dohong remained on display. However, displaying Dohong was just as wrong as displaying Ota Benga—more wrong actually, because Ota Benga agreed to appear in the zoo whereas Dohong's presence was entirely coerced.

In the United States, as elsewhere, zoos continue to capture animals. Worldwide the vast majority of aquaprison inmates have been captured. Nonhumans taken from natural environments are kidnapped. But nonhumans born in captivity also are captives, no matter how many generations of ancestors have preceded them in captivity.

Like zoos and aquaprisons, circuses falsely imprison. They also entail involuntary servitude and, commonly, battery and torture.

Much vivisection constitutes torture. Only speciesism allows people to see the torture of humans as evil but the torture of nonhumans as morally acceptable. A desire for information doesn't justify nonhuman torture any more than it justifies human torture. Even at its least cruel, nonhuman vivisection is as immoral as vivisection on Jews, blacks, mentally disabled humans, or any other humans. Vivisection imprisons, torments, and kills innocent individuals. A moral wrong is no less wrong when the victims are nonhuman. Vivisection is wrong because it's unjust.

Humane Methods of Slaughter Act

Just as the AWA sanctions the pet trade, nonhuman exhibition, and vivisection, the Humane Methods of Slaughter Act (HMSA) sanctions food-industry slaughter.

In parallel to cruelty statutes and the AWA, the HMSA doesn't cover most of the animals slaughtered by the U.S. food industry. The HMSA is restricted to mammals.

Much U.S. slaughter occurs at sea. In 2002 the U.S. commercial "catch" consisted of fishes whose collective weight exceeded eight billion pounds, as well as crabs, shrimps, clams, squids, and other invertebrates weighing more than a billion pounds.[42] Those figures don't include billions of non-targeted animals who also were caught.

Animals still alive after being brought on board are killed with no concern for their suffering. On trawlers, for example, smaller fishes are dumped onto chopped ice; most suffocate or are crushed to death by layers of fishes who follow. Larger fishes tumble onto deck. Fishes of all sizes are stabbed with short, spiked rods and thrown into separate piles by species. Next they have their throat and belly slit, in either order, whether or not they're still conscious.

Many U.S. hens exploited for their eggs don't go to slaughter. Instead they're killed at the egg factory when their laying declines. The killing methods include grinding up hens alive (for example, in wood-chipping machines), breaking their neck or back, suffocating them with carbon dioxide (CO_2 asphyxiation is slow and painful when the gas gradually permeates an area, such as a typical hen-confinement building), and burying them alive.[43]

Ten billion animals were killed in U.S. slaughterhouses in 2003.[44] The vast majority—8.7 billion—were chickens.[45] Turkeys ranked third in number slaughtered: 268 million.[46] In U.S. slaughterhouses, chickens and turkeys are foot-shackled to a conveyor line from which they hang upside down—flapping, defecating, and crying out. Sometimes, instead of adjusting the shackles to fit the legs of larger birds, slaughterhouse employees break the birds' legs to make them fit inside the shackles. Usually, the conveyor carries chickens and turkeys to a bath of electrified saline. Heads submerged, the birds pass through. The charged liquid shocks and paralyzes them but leaves them conscious. They feel the mechanized or human-wielded blade that slits their throat. Except for those whom the blade misses. These birds, and the many allowed too little time for blood loss, enter the scalding tank still conscious.[47] Some slaughterhouse employees commit sadistic acts, such as dismembering conscious birds or dropping them into the scalding tank.[48]

Among those killed in U.S. slaughterhouses in 2003, catfishes were second-highest in number: 363 million.[49] In slaughterhouses, catfishes usually are paralyzed by a surge of electricity sent through the water in their container. Because the current isn't directed through their brain, they feel a shock. If the current is too weak, they're also conscious when a band saw or other blade cuts off their head.

Tens of millions of trouts also die each year in U.S. slaughterhouses.[50] They're dumped into a mix of water and ice. Struggling to breathe, they suffer until lack of oxygen renders them unconscious in about 10 minutes. The mix is drained of water, and the trouts suffocate.

Salmons, ducks, and geese are among the millions of other fishes and birds slaughtered without HMSA coverage. Invertebrates such as shrimps and clams also are killed by whatever methods the flesh industry finds most profitable.

The HMSA ostensibly mandates that "livestock" in federally inspected slaughterhouses be killed "humanely." In 2003 these mammals included, among millions of others, 36 million cattle and 100 million pigs.[51]

The HMSA approves two methods of slaughter: (1) rapidly rendering an animal "insensible to pain" (as by a blow, gunshot, or electrical stunning) before shackling and hoisting them or slitting their throat; (2) leaving an animal fully conscious, as required in kosher slaughter, and killing them with a single knife stroke that severs both carotid arteries.[52]

In practice, much kosher slaughter is extremely cruel. Because stunning is forbidden, any cattle or other animals who are shackled and hoisted before having their throat slit are conscious at the time. Slaughterers clamp a chain around one or two of their legs and yank them into the air, where they hang upside down. This method inflicts pain, especially on heavy cattle, whose bones often dislocate or break under the strain. Even if animals aren't hoisted, they suffer the pain of having their throat slit.

Most mammals, however, are slaughtered by nonkosher methods. They're supposed to be rendered "insensible to pain" before being cut. Killed proficiently, cattle die when a slaughterer holds a captive-bolt pistol to their forehead and shoots a steel rod into their brain—once. But the pistol often lacks adequate air pressure, and slaughterers frequently aim poorly. Numerous cattle feel repeated slams of the rod. Many are conscious when shackled by one rear leg and hoisted. To end a hoisted cow's frantic kicking, slaughterhouse employees sometimes cut off the lower part of the cow's front legs. Cattle commonly are knifed in a way that fails to slit their throat. In any case, the line moves too quickly for blood loss to render cattle unconscious. Within seconds—conscious or not—they're being skinned. Even when the lower third of each leg is cut off, many cattle are conscious.[53]

Electrodes held to the head and back supposedly stun pigs and cause cardiac arrest. The electrodes often are placed incorrectly, if applied at all. Also, slaughterhouses routinely keep the current too low; instead of being stunned, pigs feel electric shock, often accompanied by the type of pain suffered during a heart attack. Even after three or more shocks, many pigs are conscious. Some pigs are beaten on the head with a metal pipe until they're dazed or dead. Paralyzed or flailing, others remain conscious while they're shackled and hoisted by one rear leg; they feel the slaughterer slash their jugular vein or cut them elsewhere. Rushed along, many pigs are conscious when they enter the scalding tank.[54]

As in bird slaughterhouses, some workers in mammal slaughterhouses treat their victims sadistically. Some slaughterhouse employees have tortured cows by shoving a broomstick up their anus or shooting out their eyes. Some have tortured pigs by slicing off their nose and rubbing brine into the wound, cutting out their eyes, or chasing them into the scalding tank.[55]

The slaughter of animals not covered by the HMSA is horrifically cruel. But so is the slaughter of animals covered by the Act. The HMSA isn't enforced.

What if slaughter were freed (miraculously) of all terror and pain? Like any other needless killing of innocent beings, it still would be immoral. Humans don't need to eat flesh or other body parts. Unlike lions and sharks, we aren't carnivores. We thrive as pure vegetarians (vegans), who consume very little saturated fat and zero cholesterol. In fact, whereas veganism promotes human health and longevity, consumption of animal-derived food increases the risk of diabetes, osteoporosis, arteriosclerosis, heart disease, and various cancers. Also, a vegan diet is the most land- and fuel-efficient. Raising crops directly for human consumption maximizes the human food supply.

The HMSA sanctions mass murder. In addition to being innocent, the victims are young—virtually all of them, not just the obvious babies such as lambs and calves. In nature, channel catfishes can live 40 years; in the flesh industry, they're usually slaughtered before they're two. Pigs can live 22 years; most are slaughtered at five to six months of age. Chickens can live at least 15 years; when slaughtered, the vast majority are six weeks old. Slaughtering nonhumans is like murdering children.

Worldwide, the law categorizes nonhumans as human property. Like other countries' laws, U.S. law is old-speciesist. Touted as protecting nonhumans, "animal" laws that authorize exploitation actually perpetuate abuse. "Conservation" laws such as the MMPA and ESA are designed to keep nonhuman populations large enough to exploit. State cruelty statutes allow all of the standard practices, from sport fishing to "animal agriculture," that terrorize, hurt, and kill countless nonhumans. The AWA endorses the sale, exhibition, and vivisection of nonhuman beings. The HMSA legitimizes unnecessary and cruel slaughter. By defining nonhumans as property, the law sanctions their abuse and murder.

U.S. law is even more speciesist than the U.S. public. Most U.S. residents believe that it's wrong to kill animals for their pelts, but the pelt industry is legal. Most believe that it's wrong to hunt animals for sport, but sport hunting is legal. Two-thirds believe that nonhumans have as much "right to live free of suffering" as humans, but vivisection, food-industry enslavement and slaughter, and other practices that cause severe, prolonged suffering are legal.[56]

Human survival doesn't require the imprisonment, forced labor, or systematic murder of nonhumans. Apart from extraordinary circumstances, killing or otherwise harming a nonhuman should be illegal.

"Animal" laws that endorse exploitation and other abuse are slave laws, instruments of speciesist oppression. As with the laws that codified African-American enslavement, justice will bring their nullification.

4

Old-Speciesist Advocacy

Most organizations that consider themselves animal rights actually conduct old-speciesist campaigns. Rather than advancing nonhuman emancipation, these campaigns perpetuate nonhumans' property status. Directly or indirectly, they sanction nonhuman exploitation. Old-speciesist advocacy includes appeals to human self-interest, language that trivializes or legitimizes abuse of nonhumans, and "welfarism," which seeks to modify, rather than end, some form of speciesist exploitation.

Human Self-Interest

Opposing speciesist practices without focusing on their immorality is old-speciesist. It conveys the message that only humans matter. Arguments based on human self-interest imply that it's morally acceptable to harm nonhumans if harming them benefits humans.

Many nonhuman advocates argue that vivisection is poor science, a fundamentally unsound, inefficient way of seeking insights into human health. It *is*. Because species differ in anatomy and physiology, observations in nonhumans can't provide a valid basis for conclusions about humans. To what extent do particular findings in mice, dogs, or other nonhumans apply to humans? No one can know without comparing the nonhuman data to the corresponding human data. But if the human data are available, the nonhuman data are superfluous. In lieu of human data, nonhuman data are dangerously unreliable. Eighty percent of drugs fail human trials after passing "animal" tests. In humans the drugs prove ineffective or harmful.[1] Other research methods are more scientifically valid and useful than vivisection. Educating people about disease prevention, increasing their access to medical treatment, and conducting benign human-based research are the most cost-effective ways to improve human health.

However, the scientific-utilitarian argument against vivisection indicates that vivisection should be judged in terms of its validity and cost-effectiveness. That message undermines the very notion of nonhuman rights. To vivisection's victims, there is only cost. Any benefit goes to individuals other than those who are vivisected.

In many ways, African-American enslavement benefited Southern slaveholders and Northerners. Did that justify the enslavement? Just as human slavery is morally wrong, vivisection is wrong, however beneficial to some. That's the message nonhuman advocates should convey.

Democratic law doesn't allow humans to violate other humans' basic rights for utilitarian reasons. Cost-benefit analyses come into play only beyond the level at which fundamental human rights have been respected. Nonhumans deserve equal justice. Vivisection violates their basic moral rights, so vivisection is unjust. The only acceptable nonhuman experimentation is clinical experimentation aimed at helping the subjects themselves.

We have no moral right to seek information by harming others. As George Bernard Shaw pointed out, the law restricts the pursuit of knowledge to methods that don't violate human rights, even though human vivisection would be far more scientifically valid (and therefore useful) than nonhuman vivisection. Shaw challenged, "If a guinea pig may be sacrificed for the sake of the very little that can be learnt from it [sic], shall not a man be sacrificed for the sake of the great deal that can be learnt from him?"[2]

Nonhuman vivisection harms innocent beings. Nearly always it restricts them to highly confining environments. Routinely it inflicts pain, physical injury, and extreme deprivation. Usually it entails death. Vivisection harms individuals who pose no threat. It isn't the kind of act that the law regards as self-defense.

If it's wrong to vivisect a human, whatever their mental capacity, it's just as wrong to vivisect a mouse. To be morally consistent, anyone who supports mouse vivisection on the grounds that humans are intellectually superior to mice must also support vivisection on humans with less mental capacity than a mouse.

It's wrong to vivisect humans because doing so causes them to suffer and die. It violates their rights. It's wrong to vivisect nonhumans for the same reasons. The main argument against vivisection should be the animal rights one.

Similarly, emancipationists should focus on cruelty and injustice when arguing against human consumption of animal-derived food products. Yes, being vegan confers numerous health benefits. Yes, the flesh, egg, and milk industries devastate the environment. Yes, veganism maximizes the human food supply. However, arguments centered on human health, the environment, or global human hunger imply that commercial fishing, "animal agriculture," and "aquaculture" would be morally acceptable if their benefits to humans outweighed their costs (also to humans). The inherent injustice of food-industry captivity and slaughter is downplayed or left unacknowledged.

In some ways, African-American slavery harmed slaveholders. For example, slaveholders became dependent on slaves' labor and skills. But 19th-century abolitionists didn't focus on slavery's costs to slaveholders or to Americans in general. They focused on slavery's immorality. Even if the Holocaust had occurred after environmentalism became mainstream, would anyone have opposed it on the grounds that gas chambers polluted the environment?

If it's wrong to kill a human and eat their remains, or wrong to do so unless you're starving, it's also wrong to kill a chicken, catfish, or pig and eat *their* remains. Except under extraordinary circumstances, humans don't need to eat any food from nonhumans.

Speciesist practices are wrong because they're unjust to nonhumans. Arguments based on human self-interest suggest otherwise.

As Gary Francione has observed, utilitarian arguments against speciesist practices shift the focus from justice (for nonhumans) to assessments of risk (to humans).[3] They take us down a never-ending road of cost-benefit analyses, immoral calculations as to which injustices and cruelties genuinely benefit humans (and, sometimes, relatively favored nonhumans such as pets).

Also, such arguments must be tailored to each form of speciesist abuse. The utilitarian arguments against vivisection or commercial fishing differ from those against hunting or "animal agriculture." They even differ depending on the nonhuman species involved, particular food involved, type of experiment involved, and so on. In contrast, arguments based on nonhumans' moral rights apply to every form of speciesist abuse.

Animal rights advocates shouldn't be drawn into debating the "merits" of a moral wrong. They simply should explain why it *is* wrong.

Speciesist Language

Social movements often involve a conscious attempt to replace exploitive, disrespectful language with language that fosters equality. For example, the women's movement has worked to rid English of gender bias. Nonhuman advocates also have effected linguistic change. Still, much of their language remains old-speciesist.

Dictionaries define vivisection as the harmful use of nonhuman animals in research. When nonhuman advocates object to "biomedical research," "animal research," or "animal experimentation," they're actually objecting to vivisection. *Biomedical research* is a misnomer for vivisection. Only some (not most) vivisection pursues medical goals. Also, biomedical research encompasses numerous research methods, such as epidemiology, use of cell and tissue cultures, and clinical studies of human and nonhuman patients. "Animal" research, too, includes morally acceptable clinical research aimed at helping nonhuman patients. *Vivisection* is the most precise term for harmful experimentation on nonhumans. Yet, most nonhuman advocates, including some who work for "antivivisection" societies, now avoid the term.

While employed by the Humane Society of the United States, Jonathan Balcombe publicly criticized use of the word *vivisection*, calling the term "inflammatory." Referring to vivisectors as "scientists," he remarked that they prefer the terms *biomedical research* and *animal research*.[4] Of course vivisectors prefer those positive-sounding terms. Bioethicist Andrew Rowan has recommended abandoning the word *vivisection* because it has "vile" connotations of torture.[5] Vivisection commonly involves torture. Because it unjustly harms innocent beings, it always is vile.

The term *biomedical research* serves vivisectors' PR purposes. It rewrites suffering and death as healing (*medical*) and life (*bio*). The

Foundation for Biomedical Research and National Association for Biomedical Research—vivisection-promotion groups—aren't about to call themselves the "Foundation for Vivisection" or "National Association for Vivisection." Whereas *vivisection* appropriately evokes moral revulsion and images of maimed and suffering nonhumans, the terms *scientist*, *biomedical*, and *research* lend respectability. Such euphemisms are both misleading and speciesist. Nonhuman advocates are the last people who should be using them. If humans were being vivisected, opponents wouldn't sanitize the practice.

Similarly, if healthy, homeless humans were rounded up and killed, no one would call the killing facilities "shelters." But many nonhuman advocates use that euphemism. Many also refer to homeless dogs, cats, and other nonhumans as "surplus," as if they were unsold inventory.

At the national conference Animal Rights 2002, UPC president Karen Davis spoke of chickens and other birds enslaved for food. The problem, she said, is that they're considered poultry. At the same time, she calls her group "United Poultry Concerns." The term *poultry* demeans birds and legitimizes their exploitation, by labeling them food. It's no more necessary or moral for humans to eat chickens, turkeys, ducks, or geese than it is for us to eat eagles or herons. *Poultry* suggests otherwise; it indicates that members of certain bird species are *meant* to provide humans with food.

Many nonhuman advocates regularly use such speciesist category labels, which perpetuate exploitation by making it sound natural and inevitable, as if it arose from the victims' own traits. Some of these labels turn a nonhuman's place of confinement into an adjective that seems to describe the victim: *circus elephant*, *dairy cow*, *farm animal*, *lab animal*, *zoo animal*. In the case of other labels, the modifier characterizes the victim in terms of their use: *broiler chicken*, *food fish*, *game animal*, *veal calf*. In reality, any elephant currently exploited in a circus or zoo could be freed from that exploitation, and no calf must become "veal."

The speciesist term *companion animal* is popular among nonhuman advocates. Fully as much as *food animal* or *game animal*, *companion animal* reduces a nonhuman to the role that they fill for humans. Like my companion Cheshie, who is a cat, I'm a companion. But no one calls me a "companion animal," partly because I'm more than a companion. So is Cheshie or any other nonhuman. There are human companions and nonhuman companions, but no companion humans or companion nonhumans. *Companion animal* implies that a dog or cat who isn't providing some human with companionship has no right to exist: their "job" is to be a companion. Moreover, *companion animal* restricts *animal* to nonhumans, even though humans too can be companions. *Nonhuman companion* avoids these problems. So does *pet*, a term that many nonhuman advocates shun. Meaning "an animal kept for amusement or companionship,"[6] *pet* indicates a nonhuman's situation without labeling them of a certain type. The word can be applied to any nonhumans, from tarantulas to cockatoos, without suggesting anything about their natures. Further, *pet* has appropriately negative connotations. Most pets aren't viewed or treated as equals, as genuine companions. Instead they're bred, sold, bought, mistreated, and, often, discarded. Unlike *pet store*, *companion store* would be a euphemistic oxymoron.

Like *companion animal*, the euphemism *farmed animal* now pervades nonhuman advocacy. In 2001 UPC, Animal Place, and the Association of Veterinarians for Animal Rights (AVAR) sponsored a conference called "Farmed Animal Well-Being." That title is an oxymoron. Under the best of circumstances, animals exploited for their milk, eggs, or flesh are held captive, genetically and otherwise manipulated, deprived of natural environments and communities, and, in most cases, killed. They can't have well-being. And they're enslaved and slaughtered, not farmed. "Farmed" sounds so benign. Would we ever say that humans imprisoned and killed for their flesh were "farmed"? No. Then, we shouldn't say that *other* animals are farmed. *Farmed* further falsifies by evoking an image of a traditional farm. Today few "farmed animals" are kept on farms. The vast majority live in crowded confinement. Finally, *farmed* equates nonhumans with plants. Chickens, catfishes, and pigs aren't vegetables; they're thinking, feeling individuals.

In *Introduction to Animal Rights*, Francione objects to racist and sexist language and makes a noticeable effort to avoid sexist language.[7] Citing a reference to a male dog as "it," he states, "Our moral confusion about animals [*sic*] manifests itself even in our language."[8] At the same time, the book is riddled with speciesist language. Francione continually euphemizes speciesist abuse (*animal agriculture, fish farms, game ranches...*).[9] He repeatedly labels nonhumans exploitable and disposable (*surplus animals, fur animals, poultry...*).[10] Throughout he uses the speciesist phrase *humans and animals*, which removes humans from animalkind. His language preserves a traditional speciesist hierarchy: "animals, including mammals, birds, and *even* fish, possess considerable intelligence" (emphasis added).[11] Animal rights books garble their own message when their language communicates speciesism.

Many advocacy groups should change their names if they wish to promote nonhuman rights. "Humane Farming Association" suggests that enslaving and slaughtering nonhumans for food can be humane. "Farm Animal Reform Movement" indicates that "animal agriculture" should be reformed rather than abolished. "United Poultry Concerns" sounds like a bird-flesh company.

Nonhuman advocates also should avoid cutesy puns and clichés that trivialize nonhuman suffering and death. The title "A Boiling Issue to Chew Over" undercuts an article that protests cruelty to lobsters.[12] The article titles "They Eat Horses, Don't They?" and "You Can Lead a Horse to Slaughter" invite readers to smirk at horse slaughter.[13] Chanting "Don't gobble me," or holding a banner that declares "Thanksgiving is murder on turkeys," makes light of turkeys' mass murder. Can you imagine early civil-rights activists holding the banner "Lynching is murder on Negroes"? Would anyone have found that amusing? Maybe the Ku Klux Klan would have. There's nothing amusing about nonhuman suffering and death. Treating it less seriously than human suffering and death is speciesist.

Finally, nonhuman advocates should eschew religious language that conveys a proprietary, condescending view of nonhumans. Judaism and Christianity anthropomorphize "God" as a man ("the Lord," "our King," "Jesus Christ"). The stance toward nonhuman animals is patriarchal. All beings form a hierarchy, and nonhuman animals are at the bottom. Speaking of "God's creatures" casts other animals as possessions: they belong to God and, through His bestowal, to humans. God has designated them for human care and use. "Dominion" over other animals (or even "stewardship") positions nonhumans as our inferiors, in need of tending and supervision. Instead, other animals need to be liberated from human interference and control. At best, the Judeo-Christian stance toward nonhuman animals is "welfarist" rather than egalitarian and emancipationist. Quoting the Bible evokes old-speciesist doctrine.

Language that transmits old-speciesist attitudes impedes nonhuman emancipation. It makes no sense to call for justice in language that legitimizes oppression.

"Welfarism"

Like speciesist language, "welfarism" impedes nonhuman emancipation. Explicitly or implicitly, "welfarists" promote the notion that enslaved and slaughtered animals can have well-being (welfare). Genuine welfare is incompatible with enslavement, slaughter, and other abuse. For this reason, I place the term *welfare* inside negating quotation marks when the context is speciesist harm.

"Welfarists" seek to change the way nonhumans are treated within some system of speciesist abuse. They work to modify, rather than end, the exploitation of particular nonhumans. In effect, "welfarists" ask that some form of abuse be replaced with a less cruel form. In contrast, rights advocates oppose exploitation itself. As Francione has written, a rights advocate "rejects the regulation of atrocities and calls unambiguously and unequivocally for their abolition."[14]

"Welfarism" is comparable to seeking better treatment of enslaved humans rather than their emancipation. It's old-speciesist because it doesn't seek emancipation or legal rights for any nonhumans. Instead it accepts keeping nonhumans within some situation that violates their moral rights—such as vivisection or "animal agriculture." Even if advocates of a "welfarist" measure *believe* that nonhumans have moral rights and should have legal ones, their *advocacy* is old-speciesist.

Participating in Abuse

In 2003 Humane Society International (HSI) instructed Jennifer Felt, its program manager for Latin America and the Caribbean, to participate in steer slaughter. Apparently, HSI decided that killing steers would boost Felt's "credibility" and her "understanding of humane slaughter." Felt killed at least three steers.[15] When nonhuman advocates learned of Felt's actions, some defended them as part of an effort to reduce nonhuman suffering. Others, including some who condone "humane slaughter" campaigns, disapproved. Felt simply carried "welfarism" to its conclusion. She directly participated in the abuse sanctioned by "humane slaughter" campaigns. She acted out the idea of "humane slaughter." Felt did what she advocates. In my view, people shouldn't advocate anything that they *aren't* willing to do themselves. If killing innocent beings is wrong, it's wrong whoever does it. Felt was morally wrong but morally consistent. Her job entails promoting "the economic benefits of humane slaughter."[16] She assists the flesh industry by informing people how to slaughter nonhumans more profitably. What if the victims were unwanted children? Would Felt participate in the killing? Would she tout the economic benefits of killing children more "humanely"? Of course not. If anything, she'd protest the killing or try to intervene. Instead of advocating veganism, Felt purveys slaughter (however "humane"). Her actions demonstrate "welfarism" at its most blatant.

Instead of enslaving or murdering nonhumans directly, many advocates promote products of enslavement and murder. For example, they encourage people to buy eggs from "free-range" hens and flesh from "humanely raised" cows and pigs. It's true that these animals generally suffer less than ones raised in torturously small cages and stalls, but they too are manipulated (genetically and otherwise), held captive, and killed. In 2003 the Animal Welfare Institute (AWI) promoted, and received part of the proceeds from, a dinner that featured body parts—including portions of ears, feet, and heads—from "humanely raised" pigs. By advertising the event, AWI encouraged people to eat pig remains. However well-housed and well-fed, the killed pigs were victims of enslavement and murder. AWI endorsed, and profited from, that enslavement and murder.

Replacing a Cruel Practice with a Less Cruel One

Other "welfarist" campaigns ask that enslavement and murder become less cruel. People for the Ethical Treatment of Animals (PETA) pressured McDonald's, Burger King, and Wendy's to require that their egg and flesh suppliers adhere to less-cruel standards of confining, feeding, and slaughtering nonhumans. These restaurants now have specified, among other things, that their suppliers must increase the space allotted to a caged hen from 48 square inches (about half a letter-size sheet of paper) to at least 67 square inches. A hen certainly has a moral right not to be confined to 48 square inches of space, but she also has a right not to be confined to 67 square inches. Confining a hen, for exploitive purposes, to any amount of space violates her fundamental right to liberty. Allotting a hen slightly more cage space replaces one violation of rights with another (albeit, slightly less cruel). For this reason, such "welfarist" measures are anti-rights.

"Welfarist" campaigns suggest that the problem lies in specific abuses (such as excruciatingly small cages) rather than the whole needless, unjust enterprise of exploiting nonhumans for food. They keep the focus off genuine freedom. The goal becomes slightly less horrendous prison conditions—room to flap one's wings, space to turn around, 67 square inches of space instead of 48—rather than release from false imprisonment. Until nonhuman advocates demand emancipation and stop sending mixed messages, emancipation will be endlessly deferred.

When PETA applauds McDonald's, Burger King, and Wendy's for buying flesh and eggs from particular suppliers, it gives positive publicity to companies rooted in the sale of flesh. This publicity encourages people to patronize those restaurants and eat animal-derived food.

In a 2000 Zogby America poll of 1,204 U.S. adults, 81 percent of respondents indicated that they'd willingly pay more for eggs from hens kept under better conditions.[17] Many people feel better about eating animal-derived food if they believe that the victims were treated humanely. A façade of humaneness helps companies to sell eggs, flesh, and milk.

The press fosters the illusion that McDonald's and other corporations have "set tough standards for animal welfare."[18] About 8 by 8½ inches of space for each hen? That's tough only on the hens. "The United States is dramatically improving the quality of the lives—and the humaneness of the deaths—of the cows, pigs, and chickens that we eat." That's how a 2003 *USA Today* article begins.[19] And that's an utterly false statement. It sanitizes food-industry enslavement and slaughter and comforts consumers of animal-derived food.

No doubt, McDonald's, Burger King, and Wendy's agreed to set new standards for their suppliers because they decided that the benefits to themselves outweighed the costs. After all, they've received substantial positive publicity while the expense of change falls largely to their suppliers. No nonhuman advocate should be encouraging people to buy animal-derived food, let alone buy it from flesh-industry giants. But that's the effect of giving those giants positive publicity.

Advocating "humane slaughter" is similar to advocating larger cages for hens. PETA and UPC have been asking that slaughterhouses render chickens unconscious by gassing them to death in their transport crates rather than leaving them conscious while they're shackled, electrically paralyzed, and slit at the throat. Remember the man who said, "God put us in charge over animals"? He told a reporter that he approves of some of PETA's campaigning. Asked to specify, he said, "The way they talk about the humane killing of animals. . . . Sure, the animal's going to die. . . . That's that animal's position in life. . . . While I'm sure [God] didn't want us to walk out there and stick a knife in it and watch it die for five hours, to put it down humanely, I don't see anything wrong with it."[20] The speaker is old-speciesist, so he approves of old-speciesist campaigning. Similarly, the managing editor of the conservative *National Review* opposes nonhuman rights but approves of PETA's asking KFC (formerly Kentucky Fried Chicken) to implement less-cruel slaughter. "Why not 'gas killing,' as a gentler alternative to the other stuff?" he writes, calling such a change "just."[21] Killing innocent beings is far from just, whether or not they're gassed. These two men endorse "humane slaughter" campaigns because such campaigns aren't rights-based. To the contrary, they're based on violating nonhumans' right to life. Instead of seeking measures compatible with the attitude that it's acceptable to kill nonhumans, advocates should consistently work to change that attitude. Without such change, slaughter will go on and on.

Asking KFC or any other company to implement less-cruel slaughter of chickens conveys this message: "It's alright for you to kill chickens, provided that you do it in the least cruel way." As David Nibert has stated, nonhuman advocates shouldn't ask a company to sell body parts from chickens slaughtered less cruelly; they should demand that the company "stop selling fried body parts of chickens altogether."[22] Animal rights advocate Sean Day has drawn a powerful analogy: "Gun hunting is less cruel than bowhunting, but I never would advocate that deer be shot with guns instead of arrows.

If we're trying to convince people that exploiting nonhuman animals is wrong, we have to give our beliefs some strength and integrity."[23] No human rights advocate would ask that innocent humans be gassed before having their throat slit. Likewise, no nonhuman rights advocate asks that nonhumans be gassed.

"Welfarist" campaigning perpetuates a speciesist double standard between humans and nonhumans. As expressed by Francione, treating "the nonhuman context differently from the human context" indicates "species bias."[24]

If I were in a Nazi concentration camp and someone on the outside asked me, "Do you want me to work for better living conditions, more-humane deaths in the gas chamber, or the liberation of all concentration camps?" I'd answer, "Liberation." In fact, I'd find the question bizarre and offensive. I'd regard any focus on better living conditions or more-"humane" deaths as immoral. It's equally immoral to focus on better living conditions or more-"humane" killing of enslaved and slaughtered nonhumans.

Some "welfarists" have responded, "You're the one treating the nonhuman context differently from the human one. If *you* were a hen, you'd prefer a larger cage to a smaller one." Yes, but I'd want emancipation incomparably more. Also, we have knowledge that hens lack. A hen doesn't know why she's being held captive. We do. A hen can't see the whole picture. We can. Instead of working to reduce the human-inflicted suffering of some hens, we should work to *end* the human-inflicted suffering of *all* hens.

Time, money, and effort always are limited. Activists should devote every available minute and dollar to reducing the number of victims and bringing the day of emancipation closer—by promoting veganism and building public support for nonhuman rights. Over the long term, the best way to reduce hen suffering is to increase opposition to hen enslavement, not to seek "improvements" in that enslavement.

Why not work to reduce suffering in ways that don't perpetuate the wrong (enslavement or slaughter) that causes all the suffering? Nonhumans have a right not to be needlessly imprisoned, killed, or otherwise harmed by humans. If we advocate that they be imprisoned or killed less cruelly, we act as if they don't have such rights; we convey an anti-rights message.

According to some "welfarists," advocating "humane" slaughter promotes respect for nonhumans. No, it does the opposite. If you don't respect someone's right to live, you don't respect that individual at all. You don't even *see* them as an individual. To slaughter nonhumans is to commit murder. To advocate slaughtering them—in any manner—is to advocate murder. If humans were being mass murdered, we wouldn't ask that they be killed more "humanely." We'd demand that the killing stop. Nonhuman advocates shouldn't be advising the flesh industry how to slaughter nonhumans. A campaign advocating that birds be gassed differs from HSI's direct participation in steer slaughter only in that PETA and UPC staff won't commit the murders themselves.

UPC also has recommended that workers in bird slaughterhouses receive training in avoiding sadism, because birds "need relief now from preventable suffering."[25] *All* suffering inflicted by slaughter is preventable. Slaughter is completely unnecessary. Calling for an end to slaughterhouse sadism belies slaughter's inherent cruelty and injustice. Giving humans complete power over nonhumans invites sadism, especially when the nonhumans have been designated commodities. The problem is the whole system. Focusing on sadism implies, instead, that the problem is aberrant depraved acts. Cruelty statutes, you'll remember, do the same: they relegate the primary problem—institutionalized exploitation—to the background and direct attention and resources to "unproductive" cruelty. Whenever helpless beings are left in the hands of their abusers, they're going to suffer. Attempts to reform such situations are fundamentally futile.

As Francione has noted, rights campaigns erode nonhumans' property status.[26] Some "welfarists" claim that efforts to make enslavement or slaughter more "humane" do this. To the contrary, doctoring abuse helps keep it alive. "Welfarist" campaigns reinforce nonhumans' property status: they propose new ways of continuing to treat nonhumans as property. Even when they aren't couched in sanitizing terms such as *humane slaughter* and *humane standards*, "welfarist" campaigns signal that enslaving, killing, or otherwise harming nonhumans can be morally acceptable.

"Welfarists" commonly call abolitionists "unrealistic." In their view, it's simply practical to advocate modifications in speciesist abuse. No, that's impractical—counterproductive. Modifications maintain, rather than dismantle, enslavement. To advance emancipation, we must increase public opposition to enslavement.

Expansion and Enforcement of Slave Laws

You've seen the worth of "animal" laws that sanction exploitation. Nonhuman advocates worked long and hard for enactment and amendment of those laws.

How has the Humane Methods of Slaughter Act (HMSA) helped nonhumans? Today more nonhumans are slaughtered than ever before, by methods that entail horrific suffering. Mammals are sent through the slaughter process with such haste that many of them still are conscious when they're scalded or skinned. Yet, activists try to get more animals covered by the HMSA. For example, UPC keeps trying to get birds covered.

Activists also keep asking the U.S. Department of Agriculture (USDA) to enforce the HMSA. The USDA's main purpose is to promote U.S. food production, including the flesh industry. Asking the USDA to enforce the HMSA is like asking slave overseers to protect slaves. The USDA is doing its job, which is to protect the industry, not the industry's victims.

Nonhuman advocates devoted considerable time and energy to the protracted process of enacting the HMSA, Nibert comments. "To this day" they "expend great effort to monitor its enforcement and to obtain closely guarded evidence of continued illegal and torturous practices."[27]

There's no point in asking that the HMSA cover more species or that the USDA enforce the Act. Efforts should be directed, instead, toward reducing the number of nonhumans who ever enter the slaughterhouse.

Activists also keep working for expansion and enforcement of the Animal Welfare Act (AWA). As you'll recall, the vast majority of mice and rats used in vivisection are excluded from AWA coverage. Groups such as the Animal Legal Defense Fund (ALDF) and American Anti-Vivisection Society have sought an end to that exclusion.

A 1985 amendment to the AWA directed the USDA to establish standards for the supposed psychological well-being of nonhuman primates in vivisection labs, zoos, and other facilities covered by the AWA. To date, the USDA has failed to do so. In response, ALDF and AWI have filed suit against the USDA. ALDF executive director Joyce Tischler has commented, "Here we are; it's 2003. What's changed?"[28] Exactly. Yet, Tischler persists in futile attempts to have the USDA protect nonhumans who are in inherently abusive situations.

The vivisection establishment initially opposed the AWA. Now they cite it as supposed evidence that vivisected animals are treated humanely. Exploiters of nonhumans "often point to welfarist reforms to defend their activities and to seek public support for their continuation," Francione notes.[29] Nibert agrees: laws such as the AWA and HMSA "stifle industry critics and quell public concern."[30] Due to such legislation, most U.S. residents believe "There are laws that protect animals." Indeed, many people wrongly believe that nonhumans have legal rights.

"Welfarists" commonly say, "I support anything that reduces animal suffering." The history of the AWA, the HMSA, and other slave laws indicates that legislated "reforms" of inherently abusive situations are largely ineffective. In the short term, they do little to reduce suffering. In the long term, they increase suffering by re-legitimizing exploitation, thereby sustaining the situation that causes all the suffering.

Before the AWA, vivisectors legally could torture dogs, monkeys, and other animals now covered by the Act. Today they still can torture these animals. Before the HMSA, pigs, cattle, and other mammals were slaughtered in horrifically cruel ways. Today they're still slaughtered in horrifically cruel ways.

"Welfarist" slave laws did little to restrain the abuse of enslaved African-Americans, whose most effective advocates helped them to escape, publicized the cruelty of their enslavement, and spread the conviction that human slavery is wrong. Analogously, "welfarist" laws never will genuinely benefit nonhumans. They'll continually defer emancipation by keeping the focus elsewhere. Even if a "welfarist" measure helped some exploited hens or mice, it wouldn't help hens or mice overall. On balance, it would hurt hens and mice by perpetuating their exploitation.

Bans That Leave Nonhumans within a Situation of Abuse

Contrary to what many activists believe, bans that leave animals to suffer or die—that is, leave them within a situation of abuse—aren't abolitionist. They're not emancipationist. In fact, they're inconsistent with nonhuman rights.

Because increased egg laying generally follows a forced molt, most U.S. "laying hens" are shocked into molting after 13–14 months of laying. In many cases the hens are denied all food for 10–14 days. (They may also be denied water for one or two days.) In other cases the hens are switched to extremely low-nutrition "food" for 28 days.[31] This second, recently conceived method allows hens to fill their stomachs (which probably reduces feelings of starvation) but imposes a longer period of deprivation; the industry considers it acceptable if the hens lose one-fourth of their weight.[32] Either way, the hens are starved. In a typical egg factory, thousands die. The survivors go through another laying cycle, lasting six to eight months, before they're killed.

Groups such as UPC and AVAR have campaigned against total-starvation forced molting. A ban on any or all types of forced molting would be "welfarist," not abolitionist. Such a ban—actually a requirement that enslavers give hens adequate food and water—would leave hens to be killed when their egg laying declines.

The forced-molting issue epitomizes the tradeoffs that "reforms" often entail. A ban on forced molting would mean that many more chickens would be enslaved and murdered. "Laying hens" would pass through the egg industry at a faster pace: egg-factory owners who previously used forced molting would "dispose of" and "replace" them after a shorter period. The number of hens and roosters used as breeders also would increase. So would the number of male chicks born and killed.

Even so, Paul Shapiro, Campaigns Director of Compassion Over Killing, has argued that, overall, a forced-molting ban might reduce the suffering of chickens because forced molting causes suffering and prolongs the time during which a hen lives in horrendously cruel conditions.[33] Whether or not the total amount of chicken suffering would be less without forced molting—which is impossible to determine—what are we doing when we ask that the longer suffering of fewer individuals be replaced with the shorter suffering of many more individuals? We never would say of innocent humans, "Please improve the conditions of those who are imprisoned and killed, but imprison and kill more people." Do we really want more hens and roosters living lives of utter misery and more male chicks being born only to be suffocated or ground up alive? To a rights advocate, the whole idea of attempting to calculate which causes more suffering—torturing and killing fewer chickens over a longer period or torturing and killing more chickens over a shorter period—is morally objectionable. Either way, chickens suffer and die. Either way, their moral rights are completely violated. Remember: chickens shouldn't be imprisoned in the first place.

According to an industry article on forced molting, the low-nutrition method of starvation was developed because "animal welfare interests" criticized the no-food method as "inhumane"; the new method "addresses the negative welfare connotation that fasting has with animal welfare organizations and consumers."[34] In other words, while continuing to starve hens, the industry now will claim to feed them. As a result, consumers will feel better about eating eggs.

What about seeking an ostensibly less problematic ban, one with no apparent tradeoffs, such as a ban on the caging of "laying hens"? Like a ban on forced molting, such a ban wouldn't emancipate hens from the egg industry, so it wouldn't be abolitionist. Also, it actually would involve all sorts of tradeoffs.

First, like other attempts to make abuse less severe, a cage ban focuses on one particularly cruel aspect of exploitation rather than exploitation itself, the cause of all the cruelty. Most people don't question the necessity of nonhuman exploitation, Francione comments. They question only "particular practices" within some area of exploitation. For example, they question the necessity of branding cattle but not of eating cow flesh.[35] A campaign to ban the caging of hens obscures the importance of eschewing eggs. Such a campaign encourages the public to overlook the immorality of speciesist exploitation except where that exploitation entails extreme cruelty.

Second, bans that don't prevent or end exploitation suggest that an inherently abusive enterprise can be fixed, made humane. A ban on caging hens invites the conclusion that caging (torture) is abusive but the egg industry per se (exploitive captivity) is not. Modifications to exploitation make it appear acceptable, especially when nonhuman advocates have sought and approved the modifications. I can't think of a better way to soothe the conscience of humans who eat animal-derived food than to suggest that food-industry enslavement and slaughter can be humane. That misconception enables people to tell themselves, "The problem isn't my consumption of animal-derived food. The problem is the way it's produced. I'm opposed to cruel practices like caging hens, which should be illegal. Lawmakers and the industry should make the necessary changes."

Third, a cage ban implies that cageless confinement is morally acceptable. The term *free-range hen* suggests freedom. But "free-range" hens aren't free, and most do precious little ranging. Many spend their lives with thousands of other hens in filthy, windowless warehouses. Many are debeaked because they're so crowded. Many never go outside. When uncaged hens do have access to the outside, this access often consists of nothing more than an opening to a grass-less area large enough for only a few hens. Do uncaged hens suffer less than caged ones? There's every reason to believe that, yes, in general they suffer less. However, they still suffer. They're still ma-nipulated, deprived, and, usually, killed when their egg laying de-clines. Currently in the United States, 282 million hens are laying eggs for human consumption.[36] If cages were banned and egg con-sumption remained anywhere near current levels, hens still would be torturously crowded. The best way to reduce the suffering of hens is to reduce the number who are, *and ever will be*, exploited for eggs— by convincing people to stop eating eggs.

Fourth, a ban that replaces one method of enslaving or killing with another method can make the exploitive industry more profit-able. In 1981 Switzerland set new egg-industry standards, with full compliance required as of 1992. The standards proved incompatible with caging. Did the mandated changes hurt the Swiss egg industry? No, they boosted its profits. Enslavers managed to hold nearly as many hens within the new confinement systems as within the former cage systems. Although the industry raised the price of eggs, demand for Swiss eggs increased: the public preferred eggs from uncaged hens. The end of caging benefited the Swiss egg industry. And what benefits an industry prolongs its life.

The economic outcome of eliminating caging might be very dif-ferent in another country, such as the United States, but this fact re-mains: Changing the method of confinement (or other abuse) can make an animal-derived product more desirable. A cage ban gives the egg industry added legitimacy and makes eggs more attractive to many consumers. Nonhuman advocates can't predict such a ban's eco-nomic consequences and shouldn't attempt to, just as they shouldn't attempt to calculate which of two abusive situations causes more suffering. They should oppose the egg industry's very existence. The relationship between abolitionists and enslavers must be adversarial, as it was with regard to African-American enslavement.

A ban on caging hens is old-speciesist. It changes the way that hens are held captive but doesn't prohibit holding them captive. It doesn't free hens from exploitation or prevent more of them from being bred for exploitation. "Welfarist" bans really aren't bans: they can be reworded as standards. As I mentioned, a ban on forced molting actually is a requirement that enslaved hens receive adequate food and water. Similarly, a caging ban actually is a requirement that enslaved hens have more space. Indeed, the Swiss cage "ban" wasn't expressed as a ban. Instead the law required that enslavers provide each hen with, among other things, at least 124 square inches of floor space. The effect was the elimination of cages.

Throughout his work, Francione emphasizes that property status violates nonhumans' moral rights.[37] Nonhuman advocacy, he states, shouldn't compromise those rights.[38] I strongly agree. At the same time, Francione argues that an egg-industry prohibition on caging hens can be "consistent with rights theory."[39] I hope I've shown that it can't. Whether or not hens are caged, exploiting them for their eggs is inconsistent with animal rights.

To be acceptable, Francione says, a ban on caging must result in hens being treated in a way that "completely" respects their moral right to freedom of movement.[40] That isn't possible. Exploiting hens for their eggs automatically entails holding them captive and limiting their freedom of movement. When a hen is enslaved, neither her right to freedom of movement nor she herself is respected. The only bans that are consistent with nonhuman rights are those that are consistent with nonhuman freedom from exploitation.

Although "still regarded as property" and "exploited as property," Francione further stipulates, the hens must be treated as if they *weren't* regarded as property.[41] Again, that condition never could be satisfied. The egg industry regards and exploits hens as property and treats them accordingly—as property. I find it wholly implausible that the egg industry ever would do otherwise.

A prohibition mustn't "substitute" or "endorse" an "alternative form of exploitation," Francione repeatedly states.[42] Explicitly or implicitly, a cage ban does just that: it condones other forms of confinement. As I stated, the Swiss cage ban wasn't expressed as a ban but as new requirements. That fact demonstrates such a ban's "welfarist" nature. Any distinction between a ban that permits the continued exploitation of the animals in question ("You can't cage hens") and new requirements as to how that exploitation is carried out ("You must provide each hen with at least 124 square inches of floor space") is largely academic. Francione apparently recognizes this because he expresses a caveat: It *is* acceptable to "explicitly endorse" an "alternative form of confinement" if that confinement "fully recognizes the animals' interests in freedom of movement."[43] Again, no exploitive confinement does that. Endorsing any form of nonhuman exploitation is inconsistent with animal rights.

Francione objects to proposals that endorse nonhumans' property status.[44] Any proposal to modify the confinement of exploited hens endorses their property status. So does any proposal to modify the exploitation of nonhumans within the flesh industry, vivisection, or any other speciesist enterprise.

Like a ban on caging hens, a ban on confining pregnant sows in crates isn't abolitionist. Instead of removing sows from the pig-flesh industry, such a ban alters the way in which they're held captive. Just as the egg industry isn't consistent with chicken freedom, the pig-flesh industry isn't consistent with pig freedom. After all, why are the sows pregnant? Their exploiters have bred them to obtain more victims. A ban on the pig-flesh industry *would* be abolitionist. It would prohibit putting pigs into the situation of abuse. In effect, it would say, "You can't legally breed, rear, or kill pigs for food." Such a ban would emancipate. Whether or not it freed currently enslaved pigs, it would prevent the future enslavement of other pigs (who wouldn't be born).

Francione doesn't categorically reject pursuing bans on such pain-inflicting practices as the dehorning of cattle exploited for food and footpad injections in rats used in vivisection.[45] I do. Such bans are inconsistent with animal rights because they leave cattle and rats within a situation of abuse (the flesh industry or vivisection). Their context is exploitation. If cattle enslavers and rat vivisectors are forbidden to dehorn cattle or inject rats in their footpads, they'll simply accomplish their exploitive ends by other (possibly worse) means. Nineteenth-century bans on the branding of enslaved African-Americans weren't abolitionist; they didn't advance emancipation. Nor would a ban on the branding of enslaved cattle be abolitionist.

In chapter 10, I'll discuss ways to reduce nonhuman suffering without perpetuating the exploitation that causes the suffering. For now, please ask yourself which makes more sense: to oppose a form of speciesist exploitation or to oppose, one after another, the countless abuses that it breeds? "Welfarists" are on a treadmill. While they jog in place, abolitionists walk forward.

If an advocated measure leaves the animals in question within a situation of abuse, the attempt to protect them will be largely futile. I can't emphasize this enough: You can't protect animals who remain in the hands of their oppressors.

"Animal-Rights Welfarists": An Oxymoron

Many nonhuman advocates consider themselves both rights advocates and welfarists. By definition, a rights advocate advocates rights. In contrast, "welfarists" work to change the ways in which nonhumans are enslaved, are murdered, and otherwise have their basic moral rights violated.

Some activists think that if they advocate veganism *while* advocating "reforms," they honor their belief in nonhuman rights. A 2003 UPC news release urging that chickens be gassed at slaughterhouses included these five words near the bottom: "We promote a vegan diet."[46] Otherwise the entire release was "welfarist." It contained no mention of nonhuman rights or emancipation, no plea for an end to the chicken-flesh industry, no promotion of veganism apart from the statement that UPC *does* promote it. If a World War II news release had called for improved "welfare" of Jews in Nazi concentration camps and stated, "We promote an avoidance of all Jew-derived products" (e.g., soap containing body fat from murdered Jews and lampshades made from their skin), would anyone consider the writer a human rights advocate?

Increasingly, so-called animal rights groups are avoiding the language of rights. In another 2003 news release, UPC referred to itself as an "animal protection" organization. UPC also praised another organization's "beautiful vision of 'a world in which every animal is well cared for and loved.'"[47] That may be a beautiful vision to UPC, but it isn't an animal rights vision. It's a speciesist, "welfarist" vision. Animal rights advocates envision a world in which nonhumans are free of human control and interference, not "well cared for." According to its mission statement, UPC "promotes the compassionate and respectful treatment of domestic fowl." Animal rights advocates promote an end to the very notion of "domestic" (enslaved and genetically manipulated) "fowl." They promote emancipation. Yet, Davis considers herself animal rights.

Bruce Friedrich, PETA's Director of Vegan Campaigns, similarly considers himself a rights advocate. In 2003 he noted the following as a supposedly significant advance: the National Institutes of Health have "issued instructions to federally funded laboratories about how to properly kill mice and rats."[48] "Properly kill" innocent beings in vivisection? That certainly isn't animal rights.

"Welfarists" who call themselves animal rights weaken the concept of nonhuman rights. They confuse the public into believing that imprisonment, slaughter, and other abuse of nonhumans can be compatible with rights. Someone who doesn't possess a right to life and liberty possesses no rights at all. "Welfarists" shrink nonhuman rights down to the right to move, the right to be fed by one's captors, and the right to be murdered less cruelly.

"Welfarist" guidelines and laws perpetuate speciesist exploitation by re-legitimizing it, give the exploiters positive publicity, make critics appear unreasonable, keep abolitionism marginalized, encourage humans who care about nonhumans to continue to buy animal-derived products, and leave nonhumans in the power of their abusers.

As Francione has pointed out, laws, campaigns, and society have been "welfarist" for hundreds of years.[49] Yet, in proportion to the human population, the number of nonhumans who suffer under human tyranny has steadily increased.

In addition to being harmful, "welfarist" campaigns consume time, money, and effort. Every "welfarist" action or word could, instead, be an abolitionist one.

The campaigns and language of many nonhuman advocates are old-speciesist. Appeals to human self-interest imply that enslaving and murdering nonhumans should be rejected only if harmful to humans. Speciesist language relays an exploitive, disrespectful view of nonhumans. "Welfarist" campaigns continually re-legitimize enslavement and murder rather than advance their abolition. Old-speciesist words and deeds impede efforts to obtain nonhuman rights.

The test for speciesism is simple: If the victims were human, would you be speaking and acting as you are? If not, don't speak and act that way when the victims are nonhuman.

NEW SPECIESISM

5

New-Speciesist Philosophy

Unlike old-speciesists, animal rights advocates believe that moral and legal rights should extend beyond our species. At present, however, much animal rights theory is not egalitarian; it displays a relatively new brand of speciesism, which I'll call "new speciesism."

New-speciesists advocate rights for only some nonhumans, those whose thoughts and behavior seem most human-like. They maintain a moral divide between humans and most other animals, whom they devalue.

Further, new-speciesists accord greater moral consideration and stronger basic rights to humans than to any other animals. They see animalkind as a hierarchy with humans at the top. In their view, some animals are "more equal than others."

Only Some Mammals

Although humans differ in their "intellectual abilities," they all deserve equal moral consideration, Peter Singer argues. He objects to giving humans with below-average IQs less moral consideration than those with higher IQs.[1]

Defining sentience as "the capacity to suffer or experience enjoyment or happiness," Singer advocates equal moral consideration for all sentient beings: "Sentience suffices to place a being within the sphere of equal consideration of interests."[2] It turns out, however, that Singer gives all sentient beings equal consideration only with regard to suffering—not with regard to basic rights, including a right to life.

Singer speaks in terms of rights with regard to relatively few animals: humans, other great apes, and possibly other mammals. Human slavery violates "human rights," Singer remarks.[3] Legally, chimpanzees should be "persons with rights," not property.[4] Chimpanzees, gorillas, and orangutans deserve "the same full protection against being killed that we extend now to all human beings."[5] What about *other* animals' right to life? According to Singer, "a case can also be made" (but less confidently than for great apes) for "whales, dolphins, monkeys, dogs, cats, pigs, seals, bears, cattle, sheep," perhaps "even" all other mammals. "Much depends on how far we are prepared to go in extending the benefit of the doubt."[6] Singer certainly isn't generous in extending that benefit.

Individuality

In Singer's view, the vast majority of sentient beings—all nonmammals and perhaps many mammals—are "replaceable."[7] As I mentioned in chapter 2, the worst exploiters of nonhumans regard them as replaceable. They speak of "replacement calves," "replacement hens," "replacement sows."

Singer considers it morally acceptable to rear chickens, catfishes, and other nonmammals for slaughter if they have a pleasant life and are "killed quickly and without pain."[8] Many flesh-eaters share Singer's opinion. They eat flesh partly because they believe (falsely) that birds and fishes reared for slaughter have a pleasant life and are killed quickly and painlessly.

Moreover, Singer regards it as a moral good to kill nonmammals and "replace" them with other individuals likely to live a happier life. "A wrong done to an existing being [killing them] can be made up for by a benefit conferred on an as-yet non-existent being," he writes.[9] Why does he say "a wrong"? Because murder does wrong the victim. He's advocating injustice. It doesn't compensate a murder victim to confer a benefit on someone else. A murder victim *can't* be compensated.

With regard to humans, nonhuman great apes, and possibly other mammals, Singer is a rights advocate. With regard to everyone else, he's a utilitarian. Utilitarians seek to maximize happiness in the greatest number of individuals. In Singer's case, the individuals include nonhumans. In utilitarian philosophy each individual's suffering is supposed to count equally, but no one has inviolable rights. An individual's well-being or life can be sacrificed to the "greater good." We're allowed to enslave an ox if that enslavement will substantially improve or prolong others' lives. We're allowed to vivisect a mouse if (you have to stretch your imagination for this one) vivisecting a mouse will save numerous lives. We're allowed to torture a human if doing so will give many people great pleasure. If Singer were a consistent (nonspeciesist) utilitarian, he'd consider it a moral good to kill relatively unhappy humans and "replace" them with happier ones. But he exempts "normal" humans (and some other mammals) from his utilitarianism.

Singer doesn't speak of most animals as individuals. Instead he speaks of them as if they were vessels containing suffering or happiness. In reality, no animal is replaceable. Both physically and mentally, every sentient being is unique. Every lobster, hawk, or housefly is an individual who has unique life experiences and never will exist again. Singer acknowledges, "Killing animals for food (except when necessary for sheer survival) makes us think of them as objects."[10] So does labeling them "replaceable."

A Sense of Past and Future

In Singer's view, most animals "do not qualify for a right to life" because they lack self-awareness, which he equates with having "desires for the future."[11] He contends, "It is worse to kill a normal adult human, with a capacity for self-awareness and the ability to plan for the future and have meaningful relations with others, than it is to kill a mouse, which [sic] presumably does not share all of these characteristics."[12]

"Of those animals that [sic] humans regularly kill in large numbers, fish appear to be the clearest case of animals who are conscious but not persons," Singer states.[13] Why aren't fishes persons? According to Singer, "Their conscious states are not internally linked over time."[14] Despite overwhelming evidence to the contrary, Singer claims that fishes lack "expectations" and, after any period of unconsciousness, "awareness of having previously existed."[15] That's utter nonsense. How could fishes feel fear without some sense of their future? How could they show learned avoidance without remembering their past?

Once minnows have been attacked by a pike, or merely seen other minnows be attacked, they flee at a pike's scent. They don't flee at this scent until they've had some experience of pike predation. Their reaction is learned.[16] Largemouth basses rapidly learn to avoid hooks, simply by seeing other basses get hooked.[17] They must have thoughts akin to this: "Unless I'm careful, *I* could get hooked."

Fishes of many species recognize other fish individuals, of both their own species and other species. In some cases they recognize more than a hundred other fishes for at least months. Among other things, they remember each individual's social rank, past degree of cooperativeness, and success rate in competition for mates and nesting sites. Fishes also develop and retain complex mental maps that incorporate landmarks and other aspects of their spatial environment.[18] They learn "what to eat and where to find it," whom to trust and whom to fear, with whom to mate and with whom not to compete, fish biologists Kevin Laland, Culum Brown, and Jens Krause note.[19]

Another fish biologist comments, "The learning capabilities of fish are impressive and entirely comparable with those of land vertebrates, including mammals."[20] Fishes can show "impressive long-term memories," Laland, Brown, and Krause remark; the belief that fishes have a "three-second memory" is "gone (or at least obsolete)."[21] Unfortunately, that belief isn't gone. Singer, for one, maintains it.

All vertebrates share the same "basic pattern" of brain organization.[22] For example, they have receptors for benzodiazepines, chemicals that reduce anxiety and are boosted by anti-anxiety drugs such as Valium®. The evidence is abundant and compelling: fishes feel anxiety and fear. Singer's claim that they have no sense of past and future is factually false.

Singer also dismisses birds as lacking self-awareness and therefore a right to life. Some jays and tits bury seeds in thousands of locations to which they return months later. How could they do that without a sense of past, future, and self—an awareness that *they* buried food? Some crows drop shell-encased fruit onto roads and wait for motor vehicles to run over the shells, breaking them open. Why do the crows wait if they lack a concept of their own future?

Clearly, Singer is wrong to think that only some mammals have desires for the future and that all other animals live "moment by moment rather than having a continuous mental existence."[23] Sentience *without* an ability to learn, remember, and anticipate would be extremely maladaptive. Sentient beings need to remember and anticipate in order to avoid dangerous and painful things and pursue beneficial, pleasurable ones. Even if some sentient beings did experience only moment by moment (extremely unlikely), they still would experience—which suffices to create a need for rights.

Like other aspects of consciousness, a sense of past and future exists along a continuum. Singer really is requiring a certain *level* of self-awareness: that of a normal human beyond earliest infancy.[24] Why a normal *human*? Why not a normal vulture or tortoise? Because we can't know their degree of self-awareness? Surely, our inability to know doesn't justify our requiring self-awareness of the sort found in humans. In fact, our inability to know is all the more reason that we shouldn't presume to judge other animals' degree of self-awareness.

Singer would reply that his right-to-life criteria are *not* speciesist because some nonhumans qualify whereas some humans don't. A human with advanced Alzheimer's disease may lack a sense of their past and future. If so, in Singer's view, that person has no right to life; in contrast, a normal chimpanzee does have a right to life.[25] Again, however, Singer's criterion is a level of self-awareness no less than that of a normal *human* child. This criterion clearly is human-centered and human-biased: speciesist.

An Interest in Staying Alive

How does Singer's stinginess in according a right to life jibe with his belief that the interests of all sentient beings, whatever their intelligence, should receive equal consideration? He contends that most sentient beings don't *have* an interest in staying alive: "Sentience suffices to place a being within the sphere of equal consideration of interests, but it does not mean that the being has a personal interest in continuing to live."[26] To have such an interest, he claims, an individual must be self-conscious, that is, have a sense of themselves and their own future.[27]

Singer equates someone's right to life with their consciously pre-
ferring existence to nonexistence. "Continued existence cannot be in
the interests of a being who *never* has had the concept of a continuing self," he states.[28] "In the interests" seems a semantic game, mere
circularity. Yes, if someone has no conscious interest in continued
existence, then continued existence isn't in their conscious interest.
However, continued existence can be in their *unconscious* interest, as
in the case of newborns whose circumstances are favorable.

It's quibbling to contend that someone enjoys eating, swimming,
or gamboling but has no interest in the state that makes those pleasures possible: being alive. As Steve Sapontzis has remarked, an animal needn't be able to ponder death for death to constitute a loss.
Human infants lack a concept of death, yet the law prohibits their
murder. For any sentient being, death ends all positive experience,
all opportunity.[29] Like Sapontzis, I believe that nonhumans' efforts
to escape death show that they value their lives.[30] But even if many
nonhumans don't consciously value continued existence, they lose
everything when they die.

And "everything" encompasses much more than experiences that
require normal human intelligence—such as pleasure in a refreshing
breeze or drink of water. As Sapontzis notes, "Superior rational ability . . . can make death *less* of a misfortune" (emphasis added).[31]
Other animals may feel joy more intensely than humans. Sapontzis
comments, "Next time you go to the beach or the park, take a look
around and see who is happiest and enjoying the day to the fullest. Is
it the intellectually sophisticated human adults, or is it the children
and the dogs?"[32]

We can't know the degree to which a nonhuman is self-aware or
calculate how richly they experience life. Is the pleasure that a dog
feels running through a meadow, or a lizard feels basking in the sun,
or a condor feels soaring at a great height more or less than the
pleasure that a human feels listening to a Mozart concerto? No one
can say. Also, to some extent the answer depends on the individual
dog, lizard, condor, and human.

To Singer, the death of a "future-oriented" individual is more
tragic than that of someone who lives primarily in the present. Why?
Death thwarts a future-oriented individual's "desires to do things"
not just in the immediate future but also in "the medium- and long-
term future."[33] In Singer's view, snails and day-old humans don't have

a right to life because their desires don't extend far enough into the future;[34] "I need to move from this hot, dry place" or "I want to eat now" doesn't suffice.

Killing a human can "make nonsense of everything that the victim has been trying to do in the past days, months, or even years," Singer says.[35] What about a bird who has been incubating eggs? Her death "makes nonsense" of her investment in hatching offspring. What about Canadian geese, monarch butterflies, sea turtles, and other nonhumans who travel weeks or months to reach their migratory destination? Why don't *their* future-oriented efforts count? Because to some humans those efforts aren't as grand as composing a symphony or writing a book? The goals of most humans aren't grand. Largely they consist of surviving and seeing one's family and friends be safe and comfortable.

Singer reasons as follows: Death prevents the "fulfillment" of "desires"; therefore, death is worse for those whose desires extend farther into the future.[36] That reasoning is fundamentally flawed. First, Singer assumes that, overall, continued existence fulfills long-term desires. For many (perhaps most) humans, continued existence primarily leaves long-term desires unfulfilled. Second, the more desires that someone has, the more opportunities for frustration and disappointment.

Like Singer, philosopher Mark Rowlands claims that individuals with a concept of their future lose more in dying because death thwarts their goals.[37] However, someone can *experience* being thwarted only if they continue to live. Rowlands himself gives the hypothetical example of a still-living Olympic athlete who has failed to win a medal: "Much of her life was lived for the sake of a future goal, which she did not achieve."[38] My point exactly. Many humans live for the sake of goals that they don't achieve. If the future thwarts someone's goals, that person suffers more than someone without thwarted goals. "It may be that the thing we wanted wasn't really worth wanting, and that the sacrifice of our time was misguided. Or it may be that the thing we wanted was something that we could not get, and that our sacrifice of time was futile," Rowlands remarks.[39]

The most future-oriented individuals spend so much time working for future goals that, in some sense, they don't live as fully in the present. To some extent they keep postponing fulfillment. The longer they live, the more deferred fulfillment. There's nothing inherently positive about desires. As philosopher Evelyn Pluhar has stated, "A life filled with many satisfactions of short-term desires may have more overall satisfaction value than one governed by a 'struggle for the big pay-off.'"[40]

Having a keen sense of past and future is negative as well as positive. It causes regret and worry as well as satisfaction. Individuals with the fewest desires are most likely to be happy in both the present and the future.

Finally, if Singer believes that having far-reaching goals is automatically satisfying, why doesn't he—as a utilitarian—advocate that humans who have fewer far-reaching goals be "replaced" by humans who have more such goals? Speciesist inconsistency. Singer exempts "normal" humans (and nonhumans of relatively few species) from his utilitarianism.

Social Ties

Singer has another, equally unconvincing reason for valuing most human lives more than most nonhuman lives. In his view, humans tend to have more social ties than other animals, and these ties make their lives richer and more valuable.

According to Singer, "It is not speciesist" to think that "the killing of several thousand people" is "more tragic" than "the killing of several million chickens" because humans, in addition to being more self-aware than chickens, have close "family ties."[41] Of course it's speciesist.

First, if social ties are so important, why isn't the life of a highly social human worth more than the life of a largely solitary one? As previously discussed, it's unjust to discount individuals (nonhuman or human) because they're unloved. Equitable laws don't accord less consideration and protection to humans who lack family ties or other social ties. A recluse or lonely orphan has the same basic legal rights as the most popular member of a large, close-knit family.

Second, social ties can decrease, as well as increase, the quality of a life. Social ties cause grief as well as joy—for instance, when they're severed. Social animals suffer when their social needs are unfulfilled.

Third, chickens are highly social. They can recognize more than a hundred other chickens as individuals. Their vocalizations vary depending on what they're communicating (e.g., "Here's food" or "Alarm!") and to whom (e.g., chicks, familiar hens, or unfamiliar hens).[42] When they aren't torturously confined, chickens commonly show concern for one another. If allowed to, hens fiercely protect their chicks, as roosters do their flock. Roosters sometimes will extend a wing over a hen to shield her from rain. When permitted, chickens form deep, lasting relationships. As reported by a zoologist, two hens of different breeds walked, ate, dustbathed, sunbathed, and slept together. One was elderly and nearly blind. The other was younger and could fend for two. During the day, the younger hen would guide her older companion around the garden and place food before her, clucking an invitation to eat. At night she would lead the older hen back to their roost. When the older hen died, the younger hen stopped eating, was "dejected," and rapidly deteriorated. Within a week she, too, died.[43] Whether or not the younger hen died from grief, she was the other hen's close friend.

Just as Singer values human goals more than nonhuman goals, he values human relationships more than nonhuman or human–nonhuman relationships. He states, "Notoriously, some human beings have a closer relationship with their cat than with their neighbors."[44] Notoriously? Why is a relationship between two humans automatically worth more than a relationship between a human and a cat, especially when the human and cat live together and the humans don't? I see no reason, other than speciesism, to belittle nonhuman or human–nonhuman relationships.

Finally, according to Singer's utilitarian philosophy, the most important thing is to maximize happiness in the greatest number of individuals (regardless of species). By far, humans cause more suffering than chickens do. Human extinction is probably the best thing that could happen to most living beings. Sapontzis understates when he says that humans *may* be "utilitarian liabilities rather than assets."[45] Singer himself has written:

> The animal who kills with the least reason to do so is the human animal. . . . Humans kill other animals for sport, to satisfy their curiosity, to beautify their bodies, and to please their palates. Human beings also kill members of

their own species for greed or power. Moreover, human beings are not content with mere killing. Throughout history they have shown a tendency to torment and torture both their fellow human beings and their fellow animals before putting them to death.[46]

Once again, Singer is inconsistent. As a utilitarian, he should value benign individuals more than those who, on balance, cause harm. In utilitarian terms, a chicken's life is worth more—not less—than the life of the average human, because chickens are far more benign. As Singer notes, humans needlessly cause much suffering and death (for example, by eating or wearing animal-derived products). Directly and indirectly, most humans inflict far more suffering than they ever alleviate. Therefore, Singer should think that most human lives have negative value.

So let's return to Singer's statement that it isn't speciesist to regard the killing of several thousand humans as more tragic than the killing of several million chickens. True or false?

"Superior Mental Powers"

In keeping with his views on self-awareness and social ties, Singer considers it nonspeciesist to believe that individuals who engage in "abstract thought" and "complex acts of communication" have more-valuable lives than those who don't.[47] As I previously mentioned, many nonhuman animals form abstract concepts. These animals include nonmammals such as pigeons and honeybees.[48]

To many people, human language typifies abstract thought and complex communication. Philosopher James Rachels emphasizes human language ability: "Man [sic] far outdistances all other animals in linguistic ability."[49]

As discussed in chapter 2, nonhumans have their own forms of communication, whose complexity we're just beginning to recognize. If humans outdistance other animals in human language, parrots outdistance other animals in parrot language.

In fact, some nonhumans outdistance many humans in *human* language. In English, the African gray parrot Alex requests various foods and toys; solicits information; identifies more than a hundred

objects by name, shape, material, number, color, and size; and expresses such emotions as frustration, regret, and love.[50] Another African gray parrot, N'kisi, reportedly has an English vocabulary of
approximately a thousand words, which he uses correctly and crea-
tively in both familiar and novel contexts. He also modifies verbs to
form past, present, and future tense.[51] Similarly, chimpanzees, orangutans, and gorillas have learned American Sign Language. No human has mastered any nonhuman language to the extent that Alex,
N'kisi, and other nonhumans have mastered human languages. Nonhumans far outdistance humans in the demonstrated ability to learn a
language of another species.

In any case, an individual is much more than a few select capacities such as linguistic ability. Someone (nonhuman or human) who
can't communicate with words or other human symbols experiences
the world differently—not more, not less—than someone who can.

Many animal rights theorists show an intellectual elitism that is
deeply anthropocentric. Singer states, "Other animals are less intelligent than we are," and applauds "the superior mental powers of
normal adult humans."[52] According to Rachels, "The intellectual capacities of humans are much more impressive than those of any other
animal."[53] Rowlands describes humans as "much smarter than other
animals."[54] The speciesist assumption here is that the type of intelligence displayed by most humans is the best type.

Singer values the life of an intellectually normal human more
than that of an "intellectually disabled" human or any nonhuman.[55]
As usual, he claims that he is "not speciesist" because he values
some nonhumans (e.g., a normal "chimpanzee, dog, or pig") more
than some humans (e.g., a "severely retarded infant or someone in a
state of advanced senility").[56] However, Singer's valuations clearly
use normal human intelligence as the gold standard. Singer assesses
(actually, presumes to assess) nonhumans' mental powers in terms of
typical *human* intelligence.

Singer states, "If possessing a higher degree of intelligence does
not entitle one human to use another for his or her own ends, how
can it entitle humans to exploit nonhumans?"[57] Yet, he allows humans to exploit and kill most nonhumans, provided that they do so
without inflicting suffering (a hypothetical with virtually no connec-
tion to reality). Singer bases a right to life on an animal's "mental

level."[58] Rowlands challenges: How can we designate a particular level of intelligence the cutoff for rights without being arbitrary?[59] We can't—unless prejudice enters in. Singer's cutoff isn't arbitrary; it's the level of intelligence seen in normal human children. A comparable racist criterion would be skin color no darker than that of a typical white. Some blacks would qualify, but the criterion would be patently racist. Singer would respond that skin color isn't relevant to a right to life. Nor is type and degree of intelligence.

Like Singer, Rachels reserves "the rule against killing" for animals with "fairly sophisticated mental capacities."[60] In some ways other animals' mental lives are less sophisticated than ours, in some ways more sophisticated.

In Rachels' view, "more complex" animals, such as monkeys, have a right to life; "simple" animals, such as "bugs and shrimp," do not.[61] As previously discussed, a more complex life isn't necessarily more valuable, either to the subject of that life or to others. So, why is complex better than simple? Rachels himself states, "The value of a life is, first and foremost, the value that it has *for the person who is the subject of that life.*"[62] In that case, the life of a genius so unhappy as to contemplate suicide has less value than the life of a bug or shrimp who makes every effort to survive. Rachels would say that, morally, a bug or shrimp isn't a person. That, however, is what I'm disputing.

In terms of natural history, no animals are more evolved than others, Rachels notes; species simply have developed along different paths, "in response to different environmental pressures."[63] Human adaptations aren't superior to cockroach ones, he says.[64] Human adaptations include all the abilities that Rachels prizes, such as linguistic ability. So, yes, there's nothing inherently superior about human abilities. More importantly, except for the ability to experience, abilities aren't valid criteria for basic rights.

A zoologist comments, "If cognition is viewed as a collection of adaptively specialized modules, then all extant species are equally intelligent in their own ways and it makes no sense to propose a [cognitive] linear evolutionary hierarchy."[65] While acknowledging that evolution doesn't support a hierarchical view of animalkind (including humans), Rachels states that the nonhumans who have the most right to life are "the mammals closest to ourselves in the old phylogenetic scale."[66]

In another blatantly anthropocentric moment, Rachels says that the seriousness of killing nonhumans depends on the extent to which "they have lives similar to our own."[67] He seeks to justify this stance on the grounds that humans have "richer and more complex" lives than other animals.[68] We're just beginning to detect much of the richness of nonhuman experience. Dolphins probably think more like humans than sharks do. Is a dolphin's life richer and more complex than a shark's? No one knows. It's presumption (and speciesism) to rate the richness and complexity of other animals' lives according to what constitutes richness and complexity within *our* perceptual world.

Many nonhumans have perceptual powers that we lack. Unlike us, many nonhumans see ultraviolet light, have a 360-degree visual field, or perceive the direction in which light waves are vibrating. Many sense infrared energy or variations in the intensity of the Earth's magnetic field. Through infrasound, homing pigeons can detect thunderstorms, waves breaking against the shore, and winds passing over mountains, all at a considerable distance. Cockroaches are 100,000 times more sensitive to surface vibrations than we are. Compared to humans, some sharks are 25 million times more sensitive to electrical fields—so sensitive that they can locate smaller fishes hidden in sand by sensing the electric potentials of their heartbeats.

As examples of humans who lack rich and complex lives, Rachels cites the intellectually disabled, such as those with exceptionally low IQs.[69] Clearly, his criteria for "rich and complex" are the cognitive abilities that most humans possess, such as the ability to articulate ideas. His argument is circular: more-intellectual lives are richer and more complex because they're more intellectual. Moreover, Rachels defines intellectual as intellectual in a way typical of humans. This, of course, is speciesist. We can't declare the life of the average dog (or a human with Down's syndrome) less rich than the life of a university professor. Conceptual richness is only one kind.

And how rich and complex are the lives of humans struggling to meet their subsistence needs—a situation in which many humans find themselves? I'd rather be a macaw in a rainforest or an angelfish in a tropical reef than such a human. Other humans are welcome to feel otherwise, but they aren't entitled to accord rights based on a personal preference for the kind of life experienced by fortunate humans.

Sapontzis observes that some people "place an especially high value on the things that only those with something like normal intelligence can experience," but "we cannot (logically) justify a claim that our feelings are qualitatively superior to those of other species."[70] Singer and Rachels place an especially high value on standard human intelligence and then confuse that personal valuation with moral rights. In the end, their notion of a richer life is simply a more human one, especially "human" in the way that intellectuals such as themselves are human.

Even if we *could* objectively say that normal human intelligence bestows an especially rich life, do we really think that someone with "superior mental powers" is more entitled to live than someone with weaker mental powers? In that case, someone with an IQ of 170 would have a greater right to life than someone with an IQ of 120, who would have a greater right to life than someone with an IQ of 100—unless we use the speciesist and otherwise-arbitrary cutoff of a near-average human IQ, in which case someone with an IQ of 100 or so would have a greater right to life than someone with an IQ of 40. I see no moral justification for measuring someone's right to life in IQ points.

In Rowlands' view all sentient beings have a right to life, but some have less right than others. Like Singer and Rachels, Rowlands values the life of a normal human more than that of *any* nonhuman. He refers to "the fact that a human life is typically more valuable than that of an animal [*sic*]."[71] That isn't a fact; it's an opinion.

The view that humans generally have more valuable lives than nonhumans contradicts and dissolves the very notion of equal consideration—not just with regard to a right to life but also with regard to a right to be spared suffering. According to Rachels, it's just as wrong to blind a rabbit as to blind a human.[72] However, by claiming that it's worse to kill a human than to kill a rabbit—because a human's life is "richer and more complex"—he invites the conclusion that blinding a rabbit is less objectionable than blinding a human because loss of eyesight supposedly robs the human of more richness and complexity. An unequal right to life is incompatible with the equal consideration that Rachels and Singer purport to espouse.

"Indicators of Humanhood"

In discussing his concept of personhood, Singer cites a theologian's list of "indicators of humanhood." Singer's primary criteria for rights all appear on the list: self-awareness, a sense of past and future, an ability to relate to others, and a capacity to communicate. As Singer notes, these capacities aren't limited to humans.[73] However, they're typical of humans: "indicators of humanhood."

According to Singer, a preference for human over nonhuman life isn't speciesist if it's "based on the characteristics that normal humans have" and not on species per se.[74] If that's true, then a preference for whites over blacks isn't racist if it's based on the characteristics of normal whites rather than on race per se, and a preference for males over females isn't sexist if it's based on the characteristics of normal males rather than gender per se. Why the characteristics of "normal humans"? Like all other forms of prejudice, speciesism entails narcissism. Singer regards what is typical of humans as most desirable, worthy, and important, precisely because it *is* typical of humans. As expressed by Paola Cavalieri, Singer's "plain, though unspoken, hero" is the human.[75] I'd go farther: Singer's heroes are humans like himself—those who are highly self-aware, intellectual, project-oriented, and social (for example, with "family ties"). Basically, Singer's criteria for rights are his own characteristics.

Only Mammals and Birds

Whereas Singer demands rights for only some mammals, Tom Regan unequivocally advocates rights for only mammals and birds.[76] The vast majority of living beings remain excluded.

Regan advocates legal rights and equal moral consideration for anyone who is the "subject of a life." In some places, he defines "subject of a life" as anyone with "an experiential welfare."[77] By definition, any sentient being has an experiential welfare, so Regan would seem to consider any sentient being the subject of a life. Indeed, he includes "young children and the mentally enfeebled" among subjects of a life, and he objects to devaluing individuals of ostensibly lesser intelligence.[78]

Elsewhere, however, Regan limits subjects of a life to individuals who possess "beliefs and desires; perception, memory, and a sense of the future, including their own future; an emotional life together with feelings of pleasure and pain; preference- and welfare-interests; the ability to initiate action in pursuit of their desires and goals; a psychophysical identity over time; and an individual welfare in the sense that their experiential life fares well or ill for them."[79] Now an experiential welfare is only one item on a list. Further, Regan states that subjects of a life share "a family of mental capacities" with humans.[80] He seems, then, to be requiring more than sentience, although precisely what remains unclear.

What *is* clear is that Regan confidently includes relatively few animals among subjects of a life: mammals and birds. However, he has recommended giving all other animals the benefit of the doubt with regard to consciousness.[81] The scientific consensus is that all vertebrates are conscious,[82] so Regan's doubts regarding fish, reptile, and amphibian consciousness lag behind. In fact, as I'll show in chapter 8, there's abundant evidence that all invertebrates with a brain (primary nerve center in the head) are conscious, as well as growing evidence that all invertebrates who have a nervous system but no brain also are conscious. Therefore, if we follow Regan's own recommendation that we give the benefit of the doubt with regard to consciousness, we should treat all organisms with a nervous system as conscious.

Pluhar, too, advocates a moral right to life for mammals and— "giving them the benefit of the doubt"—birds.[83] Recalling Rachels and Singer, she lacks confidence that animals "less complex" than mammals and birds "take an active interest in continuing to live."[84] I hope I've demonstrated that a conscious desire to live isn't a valid criterion for rights.

Like Singer and Rachels, Regan and Pluhar subscribe to an intellectual hierarchy in which humans are at the top, nonhuman mammals rank second, and birds rank third. This hierarchy falsely suggests that all mammals are more self-aware than all birds, all birds are more self-aware than all reptiles, and so on. Throughout animalkind, mental traits vary between individuals as well as species, classes, and other taxonomic groupings—with considerable overlap. The average anteater may be more self-aware than the average dove but less self-aware than the average owl. A particular anteater may be less self-aware than a particular dove and more self-aware than a particular owl. There's no such thing as a generic anteater, dove, or owl, let alone a generic mammal or bird. In addition to being speciesist, a cognitive hierarchy based on biological class is scientifically invalid.

Unequal Consideration

Regan writes, "We do not need to know exactly where an animal must be located on the phylogenic scale to be a subject-of-a-life, before we can know that the animals who concern us—those who are raised to be eaten, those who are ranched or trapped for their fur, or those who are used as models of human disease, for example—are subjects-of-a-life."[85] Know exactly where on the phylogenic scale? Why do we need to know at all? All we need to know is that animals possess a nervous system. With regard to basic rights, that should suffice.

Regan says that the animals who "concern us" definitely are subjects of a life, but he limits indisputable subjects of a life to mammals and birds. What about fishes, mollusks, and crustaceans who are "raised to be eaten"? What about reptiles, amphibians, fishes, and invertebrates who are "used as models of human disease"? Don't they also concern us? They concern *me*.

And what about all the nonhumans, other than mammals and birds, abused in other ways? At peak honey-production time in 2003, U.S. beekeepers took honey from an estimated 2.6 million honey-bee colonies comprising roughly 155 *billion* bees.[86] After removing honey in the fall, beekeepers give bees a less nutritious sugar solution, leave them to starve over the winter (when they won't produce honey), or kill them by pouring gasoline over the hive and setting it on fire. This concerns me.

Commercial fishing causes enormous suffering and kills more animals than the number who die in slaughterhouses. Consider trawling. A moving boat drags an enormous funnel-shaped net through the water. The tow forces all fishes and other animals who enter the net into the tapered, closed end. Any animal larger than the net's holes is caught. Netted animals are squeezed and bounced, together with any rocks and ocean debris, frequently for hours. Tumbled and dragged, the animals rub against one another. Often, fishes' scales and skin are scraped off. Trawling hauls up animals from a substantial depth. As water pressure plummets, the volume of gas in a fish's airbladder increases more rapidly than the bloodstream can absorb the gas. This causes excruciating decompression. Organs can hemorrhage from the intense internal pressure, which frequently ruptures a fish's airbladder, pops out their eyes, and pushes their esophagus and stomach out through their mouth. Hauling up a trawling net commonly produces a great froth of bubbles because the airbladders of thousands of fishes have ruptured. Maimed, dying, or already dead, unwanted animals are tossed overboard, often by pitchfork.

Regan rightly considers it "speciesist" to think that a dog's suffering should count less than a human's.[87] It's also speciesist to discount a fish's suffering. Does Regan truly doubt that fishes *can* suffer? If so, he's overlooking a great deal of basic science.

Regan lists examples of "animals who concern us": "cows and pigs, cats and dogs, hamsters and chimpanzees, dolphins and whales, coyotes and bears, robins and crows."[88] As you can see, most are mammals; a few birds squeak in at the end. Largely, Regan limits his expressed concern to those animals he confidently regards as "subjects of a life": mammals and birds. As previously noted, Regan recommends giving all animals the benefit of the doubt with regard to consciousness.[89] However, he doesn't translate "the benefit of the doubt" into equal consideration.

An Unequal Right to Life

Pluhar doesn't accord all sentient beings—or even all mammals and birds—an equal right to life. She writes, "It is morally preferable for a human to kill and eat a fish than to slaughter and barbecue a chicken (let alone a calf, a monkey, or another human). It is also better to eat clams than fish."[90] Especially given that a calf's remains will feed a human considerably longer than a chicken's or clam's, such an ordering certainly isn't equality. Once again, this is an old-fashioned hierarchy of animals. Why is it worse to kill a human or monkey than to kill a chicken? Pluhar claims that the answer lies not in animals' intelligence but their "capacity *to care* about what happens" to them.[91] At the same time, she belittles chickens' intelligence and indicates that they *do* care what happens to them: "One does not have to be tremendously bright to prefer pecking corn to having your head chopped off."[92] Despite her denial, Pluhar's hierarchy is based on human-like intelligence: animals who ostensibly possess more of that intelligence are more entitled to live.

Regan, too, values humans more than other animals. Forced to choose between saving a human and saving a nonhuman, we should save the human, he says. Why? "The sources of satisfaction available to most humans are at once more numerous and varied than those available to animals [*sic*]."[93] In other words, human lives are richest.

Regan imagines four normal adult humans and one dog in a lifeboat that can support only four individuals. If anyone is to survive, someone must go overboard. In Regan's view, it would be morally right to kill the dog because life offers more "opportunities for satisfaction" to humans than to dogs.[94] As discussed earlier, that premise is speciesist and lacks factual support. A dog may have *more* opportunities for satisfaction than a human. Some dogs have a sense of smell three million times more sensitive than ours. We can't even imagine the richness of their olfactory experience. If canine pleasures do tend to be simpler than human ones, they may easily be more satisfying and abundant.

Like Singer, Regan contends that his view is "not speciesist" because it isn't based solely on species membership.[95] It's speciesist because it's based on the assumption that human lives ordinarily have more value than nonhuman ones. The difference between the old-speciesist view that the life of any human matters more than the life of any dog and Regan's view that the life of a *normal* human matters more than the life of any dog is one of degree, not kind.

As expressed by Gary Francione, "our intuition" tells us that we "should" save a human over a dog if we know nothing about the two individuals except their species.[96] "We regard it as morally preferable to choose the human over the animal [*sic*]," he writes.[97] Saving the human accords with "our absolute preference for the human."[98] I have no such absolute preference, and I don't regard saving the human as "morally preferable." All sentient beings are equal, so saving the dog is just as moral as saving the human.

Francione compares choosing the human in "all" such situations to a physician's choosing to give the only available pint of life-saving blood to a healthy human rather than a terminally ill one.[99] The analogy isn't apt. Life expectancy is morally relevant in choosing between two individuals (at least, between two humans, whose sense of time we can most easily surmise); species per se is not.

Nonhuman emancipation wouldn't mean that "we will no longer be required to save the human," Francione comments.[100] Required to save the human? Yes, that view is compatible with nonhuman emancipation. However, it isn't compatible with animal equality. It's speciesist. We aren't morally obligated to choose the human any more than we're morally obligated to choose the dog. It would be perfectly moral to flip a coin.

According to Regan, "no reasonable person" would disagree with saving a human rather than a dog.[101] What's more, he considers it morally right to save one human rather than a *million* dogs.[102] What happened to his insistence that all subjects of a life equally possess basic moral rights? Apparently, that doesn't apply with regard to the most basic right of all: the right to life.

Regan's inegalitarian right to life also clashes with his statements about innocence and guilt. "The murder of the innocent is wrong even when the victims do not suffer," he states; only the guilty forfeit their inherent "right not to be harmed."[103] A dog is innocent. Is the same true of most human adults? Humans who eat flesh are parties to an "unjust practice," Regan notes.[104] Because he believes that birds and mammals are persons, he must believe that humans who eat flesh from slaughtered birds and mammals are parties to murder. If, in a crisis, I don't know the extent of a human's guilt (for example, I don't know whether they eat flesh) and I possess no other morally relevant information regarding the particular dog and human, I have no solid basis for saving a dog rather than a human, or vice versa. However, whereas a dog is innocent, an adult human is likely to be guilty, involved in the unjustly inflicted suffering and death of nonhumans. Therefore, by Regan's own standards the dog probably is the lifeboat occupant most entitled to live. (The same would apply to Pluhar's human, monkey, chicken, fish, and clam: if the human is guilty, any of the other animals are more, not less, entitled to live.)

Someone might object that human flesh-eaters aren't guilty because, although they do wrong, they aren't *aware* of doing wrong:

they've been enculturated to regard flesh-eating as morally acceptable. Most human adults who eat flesh know that it comes from
killed animals. Most also know that they can be healthy without
eating flesh. They eat flesh because they want to and their society
allows them to. They knowingly participate in needless harm, so I
consider them morally accountable.

Anyone who regards such flesh-eaters as innocent would have to
regard Americans who owned human slaves and Germans who participated in the Holocaust as innocent. Like most humans who eat
flesh, these wrongdoers were indoctrinated to participate in systemic
abuse. Further, Germans who refused to participate risked imprisonment, torture, and death. What perils confront humans who refuse
to eat flesh? Not "fitting in" with flesh-eaters? If most members of a
society condone harm, that doesn't exonerate the participants. If it
did, most crimes against humanity couldn't be viewed as crimes. The
Nuremberg Trials would have been unjustified acts of revenge.

Rowlands shares Regan's views on innocence and guilt: wrongdoing can reduce someone's "moral entitlements" and warrant "punishment."[105] Nevertheless, he too believes that humans are more entitled to live than dogs. In fact, he calls it "ridiculous," "absurd," and
not "sane" to consider killing a dog as wrong as killing a human.[106]
Faced with a situation in which we can save only a human or a dog,
"we all know that the right thing to do is save the human."[107] I'm living proof of *that* statement's falsehood.

In addition to being, in general, more innocent than humans, nonhumans within human society are less free to determine their own
fate. If a dog *were* in a lifeboat, it would be extremely unlikely that
their own choice placed them in that desperate situation. Most likely,
some human would be responsible for the dog's being present. This
is further reason to consider it right to save a dog over a human.

If, however, we have no personal information on any of the lifeboat occupants, we simply must choose. Because all sentient beings
are equal, we're perfectly entitled to save the dog over any of the
humans. It's no more acceptable to kill a healthy dog than it is to kill
a healthy human. Indeed, for the reasons I've given (innocence versus guilt, as well as the dog's lack of choice), it might be less acceptable.

If Regan believes that humans have a greater right to life than
other animals because they have more "opportunities for satisfac-

tion," then, to be logically consistent, he must also believe that the most intelligent human in the boat has a greater right to life than any of the other humans.

Regan states, "All subjects-of-a-life, including all those nonhuman animals who qualify, have equal inherent value."[108] However, he espouses views inconsistent with that principle.

Unlike old-speciesists, new-speciesists endorse basic rights for *some* nonhuman animals, those ostensibly most similar to humans. To new-speciesists, the moral rights of humans trump the same rights of nonhumans.

New-speciesists see animalkind as a hierarchy with humans on top. Assessing superiority in human-biased ways, they consider most humans superior to all nonhumans. Typically they rank chimpanzees, dolphins, and other select nonhuman mammals higher than other nonhumans. They also rank mammals above birds; birds above reptiles, amphibians, and fishes; and vertebrates above invertebrates.

As Sapontzis notes, moral progress occurs when egalitarian views replace such hierarchical ones.[109] Supposed superiority isn't relevant to basic rights. A superior aptitude for technology, verbal language, or anything else doesn't entitle someone to greater moral consideration or greater legal protection.

In terms of their right to justice, all sentient beings are equal. Intentional harm to a moth or crab is no less wrong than intentional harm to an innocent human. All animals not only have a moral right to life and freedom from abuse; they have an *equal* right.

6

New-Speciesist Law

Currently, new-speciesist law exists only in theory. Reflecting new-speciesist philosophy, new-speciesist law would accord legal rights to only some nonhumans, based on their apparent similarities to humans. Relatively few nonhumans would become legal persons (rights-holders).

Expanding Personhood

The legal meaning of *person* has changed over time. Legally, enslaved African-Americans were property, not persons. In an 1858 case, the will of a deceased Virginia slaveholder granted his human slaves the choice between freedom and public sale. Virginia's supreme court nullified this provision on the grounds that property can't choose its fate. The court declared, "The slave is not a person, but a thing"; to regard slaves, dogs, horses, cattle, or wild animals as more than property would be "bad law," even though "it might be good logic."[1]

Whether American women qualified as legal persons remained an issue into the 20th century. In 1931 the Massachusetts Supreme Court barred women from jury duty, for which only "persons" were eligible. *Person* lacks a "fixed and rigid signification," the (male) judges stated; in the present context, the legislature surely intended to "confine its meaning to men."[2]

With regard to nonhumans, legal definition continues to reflect prejudice rather than "good logic." To my knowledge, only one U.S. legal case, *State v. LeVasseur* (1980), has challenged any nonhuman's property status—that is, asked a court either to liberate particular nonhumans or to legitimize their already-accomplished liberation.

In 1975 Kenneth LeVasseur became a research assistant at the University of Hawaii's Marine Vertebrate Laboratory of Comparative Psychology. The lab's captives included two free-born Atlantic bottlenose dolphins, Kea and Puka. LeVasseur fed them, swam with them, and maintained their tanks. Shortly before dawn of a spring day in 1977, LeVasseur and several other people transferred Kea and Puka to a van, drove an hour's distance, and released the dolphins into the Pacific Ocean.

LeVasseur was charged with first-degree theft. He pleaded necessity on the grounds that his unlawful act had prevented imminent harm to "another," each of the dolphins. Forced to perform repetitive experimental tasks, subjected to reduced food rations, confined alone in small tanks, Kea and Puka had been in danger of dying, LeVasseur said. Puka, especially, had shown signs of physical and mental deterioration: a chronic cough, habitual jaw snapping and tail slapping, and self-destructive behavior such as beating her head against the experimental apparatus until she bled. Hawaiian law defines *another* as "any other person." A dolphin isn't a person, but property, the judge ruled. LeVasseur was convicted of theft. He appealed. The appellate court, too, ruled against him: "A dolphin is not 'another.'"[3]

Another legal case challenging nonhumans' property status is overdue. When rights advocates bring such a case, it should be based on nonhuman sentience, not human-like mental capacities. Most likely, however, the advocates will apply new-speciesist philosophy and argue that particular nonhumans (probably, members of a great-ape species) should be legal persons because they closely resemble humans in their cognition and behavior.

The best-known proponent of this new-speciesist legal approach is lawyer Steven Wise. In his first book, *Rattling the Cage: Toward Legal Rights for Animals*, Wise says of chimpanzees and bonobos, "Whatever legal rights these apes may be entitled to spring from the complexities of their minds."[4] In his second book, *Drawing the Line: Science and the Case for Animal Rights*, he argues that the nonhumans "most deserving" of legal rights have "certain advanced mental abilities."[5] By now, this should sound familiar; it echoes Peter Singer and other new-speciesist philosophers.

Autonomy

According to Wise, an animal is entitled to basic rights if they can desire, can act with the aim of getting what they desire, and have some sense of self.[6] All sentient beings probably satisfy these criteria. They pursue food, flee, and do other things that indicate some sense of self (for example, some awareness that *they* need food or are in danger).

However, Wise actually has stricter criteria in mind. He requires that nonhumans demonstrate human-like mental abilities in situations contrived, or at least observed, by professional researchers such as laboratory experimenters.

Wise treats mirror tests of self-recognition as indicators of whether a nonhuman is self-aware. In the standard mirror self-recognition test, a researcher places a red mark on the forehead of an anesthetized nonhuman. If the nonhuman touches the mark upon awakening and looking into a mirror, they're assumed to have self-recognition because they identified the image in the mirror as their own.

Wise acknowledges that some nonhumans have failed mirror self-recognition tests apparently due to visual (rather than cognitive) difficulties, such as the mirror's being too small for their body size. When the test has been modified, members of their species have passed.[7]

The mirror self-recognition test requires that nonhumans recognize themselves using humans' primary means of recognizing individuals: sight rather than, say, smell or feel. Someone who lacks a visual image of themselves, or who doesn't understand that a mirror is showing them their reflection, doesn't necessarily lack self-consciousness.

Wise's approach is beset with practical and ideological problems. For one thing, his approach makes it impossible for most animals ever to obtain legal rights. "We do not know enough" about "most species" to determine whether they possess sufficient autonomy for basic rights, Wise contends.[8] Apparently, most species are out of luck until "we" (actually, he and those who share his views) do know enough. Wise requires that a sense of self be "proved."[9] Given that there are millions of animal species, this would mean endless research.

SPECIESISM

Indeed, in *Drawing the Line* Wise repeatedly calls for more research. He heavily cites experimentation on animals held captive in
laboratories and expresses no objection to such experimentation.
Paradoxically, Wise implies that it's acceptable (perhaps even necessary) to violate the moral rights of nonhumans in order to demonstrate that those nonhumans should have legal rights—acceptable to
bring nonhumans under human control and force them into human
ways of thinking and behaving before they can be freed from human
coercion.

Wise grades animals on their supposed degree of autonomy,
which he equates with self-awareness. Reserved for humans, a score
of 1.0 signifies the highest level of autonomy. To qualify for basic
legal rights, an animal must receive an autonomy score of 0.7 or
higher. As determined by Wise, so far only six species "clearly"
qualify for rights: humans, chimpanzees, bonobos, gorillas, orangutans, and bottlenose dolphins.[10] With less confidence, Wise also advocates rights for African gray parrots and, provisionally, African
elephants.[11] Here again is the new-speciesist notion that rights should
be contingent on someone's degree of humanness: we can be confident that nonhuman great apes deserve rights, less confident that
other nonhuman mammals do, still less confident about birds, and so
on "down" the phylogenetic scale.

By ranking humans as a perfect 1.0 and all other animals lower,
Wise also casts nonhumans as lesser: not of equal value, not entitled
to equal consideration. As envisioned by him, "animal rights" doesn't
mean animal equality.

Currently, Wise assigns the free-living African elephant Echo an
autonomy score of 0.75, sufficient for rights. However, if some captive African elephants fail mirror self-recognition tests, he'll drop
Echo's score and that of all other African elephants to 0.68 or lower,
below the threshold for rights (0.7).[12] That is, he'll oust Echo and all
other African elephants from those who qualify for rights even if,
unknown to us, Echo herself and some other African elephants actually possess the required degree of autonomy.

Mental capacities and other traits vary within nonhuman species,
just as they do among humans. Individual African elephants surely
differ in their degree of autonomy, perhaps widely. Denying rights to
all members of a species on the grounds that *some* members fail to

meet the proposed criteria is illogical and unjust. It's akin to flunking an entire class because some of the students were given tests that they failed. The problem of unfairly applied criteria arises because it's impossible to determine the autonomy of each individual within a species, let alone within all species. (In reality, it's impossible to quantify the autonomy of *any* animal, including a human.)

Wise claims to assess the autonomy of "normal" members of particular species.[13] How does he know who's normal? If some African elephants fail tests of mirror self-recognition, how can we know that others wouldn't have passed? How many African elephants must we test before we claim to know that, worldwide, no African elephant possesses autonomy of 0.7 or higher? Six? Fifty? Eight hundred?

African elephants must be captive to be tested for mirror self-recognition. Wise proposes that the rights of African elephants hinge on the performance of captives. Are captive African elephants more representative of their species than free-living ones such as Echo? Isn't it the other way around? Most African elephants are free-living, and all *should* be. If African elephants obtained rights, their captivity would cease, leaving *only* free-living individuals.

Sentience is the only valid and fair criterion for basic rights. Whatever their degree of autonomy, African elephants definitely are sentient. That should suffice.

Genetic Closeness to Humans

As in *Rattling the Cage*, at a 2000 conference Wise dismissed the idea that insects might reason or ever should have legal rights.[14] I told him I knew of much evidence that honeybees and other insects reason. He requested references. The evidence I supplied included the following.

When a honeybee colony requires a new hive site, scouts (all of whom are sisters) search for a cavity of suitable location, dryness, and size. Each scout evaluates potential sites and reports back, dancing to convey information about the site that she most recommends. A honeybee scout may advertise one site over a period of days, but she repeatedly inspects her choice. She also examines sites proposed by others. If a sister's find proves more desirable than her own, the honeybee stops advocating her original choice and starts dancing in favor of the superior site. She's capable of changing her mind and her "vote." Eventually, colony members reach a consensus.[15]

Princeton University researchers showed captive honeybees food placed on a boat in the middle of a lake. When the honeybees were released to return to their nearby hive, they communicated the food's location to their sisters. No bees set out to the food. Then the researchers moved the food to the lake's far shore. Again they showed the location to captive honeybees. Again the bees flew back to their hive and told their sisters where to find the food. This time, however, many other bees promptly set out, flying over the lake to the food. Honeybees have a mental map of their environment. A water location, in the middle of a lake, didn't make sense. But the new location—on land—was plausible. Honeybees assess information, which they believe or disbelieve depending on its plausibility.[16]

To his "amazement and horror," Wise found such evidence compelling.[17] He now credits honeybees with the ability to reason. He shouldn't have been so surprised. Reasoning ability has survival value for insects as well as humans.

Nevertheless, according to Wise, honeybees don't qualify for legal rights. Why not? They're invertebrates. If they were vertebrates— like us—he'd give them an autonomy grade of 0.75 or 0.8, and they'd qualify for rights.[18] Lacking the proper pedigree, they aren't welcome in the exclusive club.

As expressed by Wise, Alex the African gray parrot "has demonstrated extraordinary mental abilities for an animal with a walnut-sized brain."[19] (Such condescension is what's small-minded. Human-like intelligence correlates more with brain-to-body ratio than with absolute brain size. Parrots actually have a large brain for their body size, as do honeybees.) Even so, Wise doesn't place African gray parrots among the animals who incontestably deserve rights. They're too evolutionarily distant from humans, he says. Their cognitive abilities may have developed independently of ours, along a different ancestral line.[20] So, even if African gray parrots possess the abilities in question, they shouldn't receive full credit for them if the origin of those abilities differs from the origin of our same abilities. That's like saying that my 2004 Honda Civic is better than yours because yours came from a different dealer.

The "taxonomically closer" a nonhuman species is to humans, the "more confident we can be" in assigning its members a high autonomy value, Wise argues.[21] Closely related species such as chimpanzees and humans do share more of their evolution (including the evolution of their mental traits) than distantly related species, but all animals are kin. Also, as Wise notes, the same capacities often evolve independently along different ancestral lines. Speciesists assume that nonhuman intelligence correlates with biological relatedness to humans. For this reason they may recognize intelligence in nonhuman mammals but not in birds, or recognize it in mammals and birds but not fishes, and so on. This is biological classism. Less closely related to humans doesn't mean less intelligent, even if we define intelligence as human-like intelligence. Octopuses apparently possess more human-like intelligence than frogs, but we're far more closely related to frogs.

Like other new-speciesists, Wise has a hierarchical view of species: human traits are the most advanced. In reality, species don't evolve toward greater humanness but toward greater adaptiveness in their ecological niche. Our species occupies one of countless branches on the evolutionary bush. Life hasn't evolved along a single stalk, with nonhumans mired at its roots and humans blossoming at its tip. Nor is species stable and fixed. The human species, like all others, continues to undergo variation. A centipede or flamingo embodies as long a period of evolution as a human: since the beginning of life on Earth.

Nonhumans and humans share now-extinct ancestors. No living group of nonhuman animals—no existing species of invertebrate, fish, amphibian, reptile, bird, or nonhuman mammal—is ancestral to humans. No nonhuman alive today belongs to the same species as some ancestor of humans. Modern fishes radically differ from the fish who was the last common ancestor of fishes and humans. No frog, toad, or salamander ever was our forebear. Although we have reptilian ancestors, we didn't descend from reptiles of any species alive today. The first lizards, snakes, crocodiles, and turtles appeared after the first mammals. No bird ever was our ancestor. Birds and mammals evolved from different groups of reptiles. Birds first appeared about 50 million years *after* mammals. Like us, the first fishes had skeletons of bone. But sharks, skates, and rays have skeletons of cartilage. If evolution proceeds toward humanness, why did some fishes with skeletons of bone evolve into fishes with skeletons of cartilage? Why did birds come to exist after mammals?

Today's nonhuman apes don't represent earlier stages in human development. Our common ape-like ancestor lived about 15 million years ago. About six million years ago, human and chimpanzee evolution parted. Chimpanzees didn't prepare the way to us any more than we prepared the way to them.

The notion of higher and lower beings lacks scientific validity. In an 1858 letter, Charles Darwin expressed his intention "carefully to avoid" referring to some animals as "higher" than others.[22] Elsewhere he penciled this reminder to himself: "Never use the words higher and lower."[23] As stated by two neuroscientists, ranking species in some linear order that suggests evolutionary progress makes "no sense" and has "no scientific status."[24]

Similarity to Children

Wise's approach is deeply speciesist, utterly biased in favor of humanness. The "certain advanced mental abilities" that Wise requires are those typical of humans. "The autonomy values we assign to nonhumans will be based upon human abilities and human values," he acknowledges.[25] "The more exactly the behavior of any nonhuman resembles ours," the more confidently we can assign them "an autonomy value closer to ours."[26]

Wise advocates assessing the intelligence of nonhumans by giving them tests designed for human children, even though, by his own admission, such tests may not be valid for nonhumans.[27] In his scheme, as in Singer's philosophy, nonhumans (and humans) are "entitled" to basic legal rights only if their ostensible autonomy equals or surpasses that of a "normal human child."[28] Comparing nonhumans to human children is unfair and patronizing to nonhumans. As you'll recall, some birds can remember thousands of soil locations in which they've buried seed. What test designed for children, or even adult humans, could reveal that?

If captive gorillas and bottlenose dolphins seem to resemble human children, it's because they've been forced to depend on their

captors and they've been placed in stultifying environments that allow scant expression of their natural nonhuman abilities (environments such as the laboratories in which Wise would see them be
tested). We're used to *thinking* of dog and cat companions as children. Even when they're adults, we scold them as "bad," praise them
as "good," and refer to them as "girl" and "boy" (the way sexist men
call women "girls" and racist whites have addressed black men as
"boy"). But dogs, cats, and other nonhumans aren't children and
shouldn't be required to act as if they are.

According to Wise, the more a nonhuman's mind appears to be
"simpler" than a child's—or "just different"—the weaker that individual's claim to rights.[29] Equating "different from humans" with
lesser is the essence of speciesism.

Contradictions

Wise's arguments are riddled with contradictions. On the one hand
he advocates applying the precautionary principle of law, according
to which the mere threat of harm justifies preventive action.[30] On the
other hand he doesn't advocate legal rights for most nonhumans,
even though billions of them are threatened—right now—with imminent capture, confinement, vivisection, slaughter, or other grave
harm by humans. Indeed, every moment of every day, at least hundreds of millions of nonhumans suffer such harm.

Wise defends his emphasis on autonomy as a response to the way
in which judges decide cases. Judges, he says, think in terms of autonomy.[31] No, they don't—not, at least, as Wise defines autonomy.
Courts regard the most mentally incompetent humans as persons
with rights, he himself notes.[32]

In fact, Wise cites a legal case in which the Massachusetts Supreme Court asserted its duty to "safeguard the well-being" and "en-
sure the rights" of a "profoundly mentally retarded" 67-year-old
man.[33] Possessing an IQ of 10, Joseph Saikewicz communicated
only through "gestures and grunts," couldn't understand words, and
apparently couldn't conceptualize death.[34] No matter. The court affirmed the "principles of equality and respect for all individuals,"
declaring that "the value of life under the law [has] no relation to in-

telligence" or an individual's ability to "appreciate" life.[35] What's more, the court referred to Saikewicz as having "autonomy."[36]

In chapter 2, I mentioned Nicholas Romeo, a man who has an IQ of about 9, can't speak, and "lacks the most basic self-care skills."[37] The U.S. Supreme Court ruled, in 1982, that he has constitutionally protected "liberty interests in safety and freedom from bodily restraint."[38] As legal scholars Lee Hall and Anthony Jon Waters have written, "Even when mentally disabled humans function only on a basic level, they are 'persons' in the eyes of the law."[39]

Compassionate law recognizes that individuals with apparently little autonomy are particularly vulnerable to abuse; their need for legal rights is especially strong. Yet, Wise advocates legal rights for only the most autonomous nonhumans.

Judges consider the well-being of young children and other humans who lack sufficient autonomy to make important decisions regarding their own welfare. In such instances the court or a guardian makes the necessary decisions, presumably in the individual's best interest. Whether or not bottlenose dolphins are autonomous in Wise's sense, when they acquire legal rights and someone violates those rights, humans will have to act on their behalf. Dolphins can't ask the legal system for justice. Humans must do that. Given that nonhumans can't plead their own case or state their preferred fate in a court of law, what's the point—moral *or* legal—of attempting to assess their degree of autonomy?

Wise says that he assesses nonhuman autonomy in terms of human intelligence because "the law measures nonhuman animals with a human yardstick."[40] The law doesn't measure nonhuman capacities. It measures nonhumans' financial and, to much lesser extent, emotional value to humans. The law regards nonhumans as property. And isn't the goal to change the way the law views nonhumans? Wise fails to provide any cogent, logically consistent reason for his severely restrictive autonomy criteria.

Also, Wise's operational definition of autonomy is fundamentally awry. Wise proposes demonstrating supposed autonomy in a way that robs nonhumans of autonomy. Fundamentally he defines nonhuman autonomy as its opposite. Nonhumans must display humanlike behavior. They receive autonomy points for performing human-devised tasks such as mirror self-recognition.

Instead of possessing the freedom to be their parrot selves, parrots must mimic human children. For decades, Alex the African gray parrot has been held captive in Irene Pepperberg's university laboratory and subjected to experiment after experiment. He lives in a completely unnatural environment, under the control of humans who radically manipulate his thoughts and behavior.

Sometimes, bored and irritated by repetitive questions, Alex rebels against his exploiters, who might justifiably be termed his tormentors. "I'm gonna go away," he announces, and he walks off.[41] Or he shouts, "No!" and turns his back. Once, asked to name the green object among six objects on a tray, Alex named every object *except* the green one. Then he flipped the tray to the floor.[42]

When Alex rebels, he's demonstrating autonomy: mental independence, a will of his own. His tragic, futile assertion of self is lost on his captors.

Wise's pseudoscientific approach would demean and coerce other animals as surely as having them perform in nightclub, aquaprison, or circus acts. Instead of receiving food or praise, the captives might "earn" fundamental rights. If the slaves sing and dance to our satisfaction, we might grant them their freedom.

Demonstrating Humanness

With good reason, Wise repeatedly compares nonhuman enslavement to the former enslavement of African-Americans. If opponents of African-American enslavement had adopted a racist approach comparable to Wise's speciesist one, they would have advocated rights for only some blacks: those who most resemble whites.

Before African-American emancipation, a number of slaves sued for freedom on the grounds that they were white. Unable to *prove* whiteness, they had to demonstrate that they were so much *like* a white that they should be given "the benefit of the doubt." These plaintiffs presented physical evidence of whiteness, such as light skin, eyes, and hair. They also presented behavioral evidence that they socialized with whites (for example, attended church with them) and conducted themselves in a ladylike or gentlemanly way associated with white respectability. Law professor Ariela Gross comments, "Doing the things a white man or woman did became the law's working definition" of whiteness. For instance, a person might demonstrate accomplishments such as financial self-support. "People described others as white or black in terms of their competencies and disabilities."[43]

Ancestry also factored in. Evidence of African ancestry counted against the plaintiff; evidence of European or other non-African ancestry counted in their favor. In one case, the judge instructed the jury to award the plaintiffs freedom if the evidence indicated that they were less than one-fourth black: greater than 0.75 in whiteness.[44]

We react with revulsion to the idea of demonstrating whiteness. We should react with equal revulsion to the idea of demonstrating humanness.

Wise would subject nonhumans to the same sort of bigoted, degrading tests that enslaved humans had to "pass" in order to receive the freedom that always was rightfully theirs. Just as demonstrations of whiteness were based on deeply racist premises, Wise's proposed demonstrations of humanness are based on deeply speciesist ones. Wise, you'll remember, considers the ancestry of African gray parrots and, deeming it too remote from ours, counts it against them. In Wise's scheme, nonhumans don't get freedom unless their ancestry is sufficiently human (white) and members of their species have demonstrated a sufficient number of human (white) traits. They don't get freedom unless members of their species have scored 0.7 or higher in humanness (whiteness).

Today, of course, no one must demonstrate whiteness in order to be free. Nor should anyone have to demonstrate humanness.

Demonstrating whiteness never had the power to free more than relatively few individuals. Although Wise's approach would emancipate entire species, those species would amount to a select few.

Making freedom contingent on whiteness maintained white supremacy; it kept whites in the position of judge and superior being. Outside a racist context, no one ever would "aspire" to whiteness. Analogously, only speciesism could place nonhumans in the degrading, oppressive situation of having to demonstrate humanness. Wise's approach would further inscribe human supremacy into law.

By requiring that nonhumans demonstrate human-like traits, and by ranking nonhumans accordingly, Wise perpetuates speciesism. His approach is harmful because it focuses on "mental abilities" rather than sentience and places the burden of proof on nonhumans, who must demonstrate human-like capacities to his and others' satisfaction. Wise's criteria for rights are substantially stricter even than those developed by other new-speciesists.

With regard to legal rights, Singer has praised Wise for supposedly answering the question "Where should we draw the line?"[45] The answer always has been far simpler than Singer, Wise, and other new-speciesists would have us believe. The line should be drawn between sentient beings and insentient things.

7

New-Speciesist Advocacy

The Great Ape Project (GAP) illustrates new-speciesist advocacy. GAP demands personhood for relatively few nonhumans, primarily on the grounds that they closely resemble humans.

As outlined in *The Great Ape Project: Equality beyond Humanity*, edited by Paola Cavalieri and Peter Singer, GAP asks that non-human great apes (chimpanzees, bonobos, gorillas, and orangutans) be legally categorized as persons, not property. GAP advocates granting all nonhuman great apes a legal right to life, liberty, and freedom from "the deliberate infliction of severe pain."[1] The project aims to breach the "species barrier" that currently limits rights to humans and thereby "establish a precedent for many other animals."[2] "Moral decisions" should be made on "valid grounds," GAP states, "not for irrelevant reasons of species membership."[3] So far, so good. There's nothing speciesist about any of these contentions or goals.

"Complex Individuals"

Some people have called GAP "anthropocentric" and "speciesist" because it focuses only on great apes, GAP says.[4] It isn't GAP's focus that I find speciesist but a number of its stated *reasons* for that focus. Stressing human-like capacities and behaviors, GAP suggests that the nonhumans who most resemble humans are most entitled to legal rights. It promotes criteria developed by Singer and other new-speciesists.

GAP states that nonhuman great apes have "mental capacities and an emotional life sufficient to justify inclusion within the community of equals."[5] *Any* mental capacity should suffice for moral equality.

Nonhuman great apes need and deserve legal rights for the same reason that turkeys, wasps, and salamanders do: they experience.

"Irrefutable scientific evidence is available now to show that [nonhuman great apes] are complex individuals with equally complex interests," GAP argues.[6] Two problems here. First, there's the suggestion (made explicit in Steven Wise's work) that most nonhumans have no claim, or only a weak claim, to legal rights until some indeterminate amount of future research has demonstrated their complexity to the satisfaction of some indeterminate number of humans. Second, there's the suggestion that complex individuals are more entitled to legal rights than supposedly simpler ones. Remember Rachels' "more complex" lives? All sentient beings are complex enough to be conscious, and consciousness should suffice for legal rights.

According to GAP, the "rich individuality" of nonhuman great apes makes them "one of the most obvious cases" of nonhumans who should have legal rights.[7] I agree that a recognition of nonhuman individuality is crucial to extending legal rights beyond humans. Personal familiarity with a species increases our ability to see its members as individuals. Having had dog and cat companions, many Westerners recognize dog and cat individuality. Because other great apes look and act so much like humans, it's also easier for most humans to recognize individuality in nonhuman great apes than in most other animals. I have no objection to exploiting that fact. However, citing the "rich individuality" of nonhuman great apes implies that they *possess* more individuality than most other animals and are therefore more entitled to rights. A particular gorilla is unique, but so is a particular seagull or goat. All sentient beings are unique individuals. The extent to which they have personalities, idiosyncratic habits, original ideas, or other distinguishing characteristics doesn't make them more or less entitled to rights.

Cavalieri and Singer address the complaint that GAP shows speciesist elitism: "It might be said that in focusing on beings as richly endowed as the great apes we are setting too high a standard for admission to the community of equals, and in so doing we could preclude, or make more difficult, any further progress for animals whose endowments are less like our own. No standard, however, can be fixed forever."[8] Whether or not a standard based on endowments is fixed, it's speciesist. And applying such a standard prolongs its existence. The very terms *standard* and *endowments* suggest that an individual must meet certain criteria to qualify for rights. Again, focusing on nonhuman great apes isn't the problem; the problem is perpetuating the view that they're more endowed, and therefore more entitled to rights, than other nonhumans.

GAP claims to focus on other great apes "not because they are human-like" but because they possess "morally relevant" characteristics: "These characteristics, such as complex emotional life, strong social and family bonds, and self-awareness, have a great moral weight not because most humans have them too, but because they are morally relevant in themselves."[9] In chapter 5, I showed that these characteristics are *not* morally relevant in themselves.

Similarity to Humans

In arguing that nonhuman great apes should have legal rights, GAP sometimes directly cites their genetic, cognitive, and behavioral similarities to humans. They're our "closest relatives," GAP notes, going so far as to call them our "doubles."[10]

All sentient beings need and deserve the basic rights that GAP seeks for nonhuman great apes. Life, liberty, and freedom from pain are as relevant to bullfrogs and snakes as to bonobos. In fact, I can't think of any basic right that applies to nonhuman great apes but doesn't also apply to all other sentient beings. Turtles and walruses don't need freedom of speech or a right to vote, but neither do chimpanzees and gorillas. A nonhuman's genetic closeness to humans isn't germane.

Other great apes "most resemble us in their capacities and their ways of living," Cavalieri and Singer state. Humans are "intelligent beings with a rich and varied social and emotional life." Because they "share" these characteristics, "our fellow great apes" deserve "moral equality."[11] No, nonhuman great apes deserve moral equality because they're sentient. Their degree of intelligence, sociability, or emotionality isn't relevant.

As expressed by Gary Francione, denying personhood to nonhuman great apes is "irrational in light of the demonstrated mental and emotional similarities" between them and us.[12] Apart from sentience, those similarities aren't relevant. It's just as irrational to deny basic rights to a wolf as to a chimpanzee—because both are sentient. After all, who believes that nonhuman great apes are sentient but wolves aren't? Indeed, it's irrational to deny basic rights to a cricket, finch, tuna, or squid unless a person is ignorant of their sentience.

Steve Sapontzis has observed of GAP, "We are called on to recognize that harmful experiments on nonhuman great apes are wrong because these apes are genetically so much like us or because they are so intelligent, again like us. Such calls clearly retain an anthropocentric view of the world."[13]

As demonstrated in chapters 2 and 5, linking basic rights to human-like mental capacities is biased and logically inconsistent. To the extent that it proposes rights for nonhuman great apes *because they're so much like us*, GAP perpetuates speciesism.

A "Dire Predicament"

GAP offers another reason for focusing on nonhuman great apes: "their dire predicament."[14] This reason conflicts with the notions that (1) rights apply at the level of individuals and (2) in terms of moral consideration, all individuals are equal.

Relative to the predicament of numerous other animals, that of nonhuman great apes is particularly dire only in the sense that their species are in danger of imminent extinction. Each year, billions of chickens are held captive in torturous conditions and slaughtered. In terms of the number of individuals who suffer intensely and are murdered, the predicament of chickens is unquestionably more dire than that of any great-ape species (including humans).

We violate the principle of equal consideration of individuals when we give members of endangered species greater moral consideration than members of highly populous species. An individual is fully entitled to rights whatever the size of their group. Their importance (or unimportance) to other beings and to ecosystems shouldn't affect their rights. A kangaroo is just as entitled to basic rights as a giant panda. To see group size as relevant to individual rights is to regard individuals as mere species representatives. That's a utilitarian, not a rights, view of other animals. It's speciesist. In fact, it's old-speciesist.

The "dire predicament" argument isn't speciesist, someone might counter, because people also apply it to humans: protecting endangered species is like trying to prevent genocide against particular human groups. It's true that international laws and the U.S. Code prohibit genocide. In effect, however, such laws prohibit mass murder of members of a particular group. Every day, humans mass-murder chickens, catfishes, pigs, and other nonhumans. To argue that nonhuman great apes have some special claim to emancipation on the grounds of genocide while humans kill millions of chickens each day is, to say the least, unconvincing.

Many judges do value members of endangered species more than other nonhumans. However, such judges could note that laws aimed at preserving species already exist. They also could recommend increased efforts to breed nonhuman great apes. Genetically manipulating nonhumans violates their rights. To have any solidity and integrity, individual rights must be independent of population size.

Claiming exigency based on the threat of extinction displays the same speciesism as the Endangered Species Act and Marine Mammal Protection Act (see chapter 3). Why wouldn't the threatened use of a chimpanzee in vivisection suffice to show exigency? And why isn't the threatened use of a rat equally pressing? If individuals truly receive equal consideration, population size neither reduces nor increases the urgency when they're threatened with harm.

There is, however, a nonspeciesist way in which the small number of remaining nonhuman great apes increases the chances of winning their rights: dealing with their emancipation would be relatively easy. Humans' current property interests in nonhuman great apes amount to a small fraction of their property interests in, say, salmons or mice. GAP believes that, initially, it will be easier to achieve rights for a relative few than for many.[15] That's probably true, and there's nothing speciesist about that belief. (Still, it might be easier to obtain rights for dolphins than for nonhuman great apes, because dolphins are more popular with the general public and aren't used in vivisection that the public mistakenly regards as having substantial life-saving potential, such as AIDS research on chimpanzees.)

If someone thinks that a great-ape campaign is more winnable than others, they should go ahead. However, they shouldn't argue based on the shared characteristics (other than sentience) of humans and other great apes.

A Matter of Strategy

Cavalieri and Singer say that focusing on other great apes enables advocates to use some of the same arguments commonly used to defend old speciesism: "The very arguments usually offered to defend the special moral status of human beings *vis-à-vis* nonhuman animals—arguments based on biological bondedness or, more significant still, on the possession of some specific characteristics or abilities—can be turned against the status quo."[16] Why are those arguments usually used to defend speciesism? Because they *are* speciesist.

If speciesist arguments work to the advantage of nonhuman great apes (and I'm not convinced of that), they do so at other animals' expense. I'm not saying that we must emancipate either everyone or no one. "Welfarists" often falsely accuse abolitionists of being "all or nothing." I know that emancipating African-Americans didn't emancipate any nonhumans. I know that granting voting rights to African-American men didn't secure voting rights for American women. I know that virtually no judge alive today would declare an ostrich or crayfish a person. But emancipating African-Americans didn't rely on racist arguments, and emancipating the first nonhumans shouldn't rely on speciesist ones.

Someone might counter, "Isn't it speciesist to deny nonhuman great apes the chance to become legal persons? GAP is just being practical. They simply want to do what will work. No matter how it's obtained, personhood for any nonhumans will be so groundbreaking that it will help all nonhumans. It will breach the legal barrier between humans and all other animals." I completely support efforts to obtain great-ape personhood, provided that they're nonspeciesist. As with "welfarism" versus rights, the question is what will work in the full sense of work—truly work for the animals in question, work over the long term, work without benefiting some animals at the expense of more-numerous others, work without perpetuating the very speciesism that personhood for any nonhumans should erode rather than reinforce. I'd sob with joy if chimpanzees became legal persons, as long as their personhood wasn't couched in terms that will make it harder for other nonhumans to obtain personhood.

Why not seek great-ape personhood in nonspeciesist ways? Why not build the foundation on which animal equality must rest? Nonspeciesist arguments advance *everyone's* interests. They're necessary for full emancipation. At the same time, they don't preclude starting with relatively few nonhumans whose sentience is especially obvious to humans.

Given current attitudes toward nonhumans, someone pleading for chinchilla, spider, or sea-horse personhood would be laughed right out of court. However, arguing for great-ape personhood doesn't require speciesist argumentation of the sort presented by GAP. As noted in the previous chapter, courts have affirmed the "principles of equality and respect for all individuals" regardless of their "intelligence" or ability to "appreciate" life.[17] The individuals in those cases have, of course, been human, but the same egalitarian principles could be applied in a legal case seeking rights for, say, chimpanzees or dolphins.

In fact, arguing based on sentience alone might be less threatening to judges than arguing based on human–nonhuman similarities. Citing abilities such as nonhuman great apes' ability to learn human languages suggests that animal rights advocates seek nonhuman participation in human society. We don't. We're not asking that any nonhumans have freedom of speech or voting rights. So, what difference does it make if nonhumans can learn human languages or show other human-like capacities and behaviors? We don't want nonhumans to remain within human society (which invariably would keep them subservient). We want them to be free and independent of humans. In some ways, that's less threatening than giving rights to a new group of humans, who then share economic, social, and political power. Nonhumans wouldn't share power. They would be shielded from *ours*.

It's right to seek legal personhood for nonhuman great apes. It isn't right to do so in a speciesist way. As currently conceived and presented, GAP reinforces a species hierarchy, with great apes ranking above all other animals.

If a judge rules that a chimpanzee is a person because chimpanzees are so human-like, yet another speciesist precedent will be set. Such a precedent would fuel the type of approach proposed by Wise. Humans continually would judge nonhumans (especially captives) by the extent to which they demonstrate human-like capacities. Such a scenario is degrading to nonhumans and frightening in its potential to perpetuate nonhuman suffering.

Instead of arguing that chimpanzees show human-like intelligence and sociability and are our close relatives, advocates should argue that chimpanzees obviously can suffer and otherwise experience. That is, chimpanzees clearly are sentient.

Nonspeciesists don't want relatively few nonhumans to be honorary humans. They want sentience to replace humanness as the basis for rights.

ANIMAL EQUALITY

8

Nonspeciesist Philosophy

Many philosophers—among them, new-speciesists such as Peter Singer—have argued that sentience suffices for moral consideration. Sentience also should suffice for legal rights and *equal* consideration.

By definition, sentient beings experience. The capacity to experience should confer legal rights because that capacity creates a need for protection. Given humans' propensity to needlessly harm other animals, nonhumans need legal rights to protect them from humans. For example, they need rights to life and liberty.

As I demonstrated in chapter 5, new-speciesist rationales for favoring humans and the nonhumans who most resemble them are unfair and logically inconsistent. Because much suffering isn't "directly related to understanding," the extent to which a particular individual possesses the understanding of a normal adult human is "beside the point," Steve Sapontzis notes.[1]

The law prohibits the torture of humans because they can suffer, not because they have language (some don't) or are rational (I often feel that most aren't). Other animals do reason, including in human-like ways, but neither physical nor psychological suffering requires human-like intelligence. Beatings hurt and hunger aches whatever an individual's IQ. Most animals will suffer from imposed immobility. Social animals will suffer from isolation. Curious ones will suffer from monotony. Suffering matters, whoever is doing the suffering.

And thought and perception matter, whoever is doing the thinking and perceiving. Each sentient being represents a mental world. Any form of consciousness should suffice to confer legal personhood.

Moral and Legal Equality

Gary Francione advocates freeing all sentient beings from human exploitation.[2] Many humans, such as young children and adults with severe mental disabilities, can't think rationally or in abstract terms, he remarks; society doesn't consider it acceptable to use such people in vivisection "or as sources of food or clothing."[3]

However, Francione suggests that, beyond emancipation, some animals might be entitled to stronger legal protection than others: sentience suffices for "the right not to be property," but "cognitive and genetic similarities between humans and [other] great apes might justify according equal rights to [nonhuman] great apes."[4] As I commented in the preceding chapter, I can't think of any human right that applies to nonhuman great apes but doesn't also apply to all other sentient beings. A ladybug can't benefit from freedom of religion or a right to petition, but neither can an orangutan. As I'll discuss in the next chapter, Francione also weighs nonhumans' moral rights less heavily than humans' same rights.

Sapontzis espouses a more egalitarian philosophy. He advocates not only that all sentient nonhumans be freed from human exploitation but also that they have equal rights—equal not in the sense of being entirely the same as humans' but in the sense of affording equal protection. All sentient beings (nonhuman and human) have equal value, he asserts; they're entitled to "the same level of moral and legal protection."[5]

In her most recent work, Paola Cavalieri too rejects an animal hierarchy. In her view, all conscious beings should receive "full moral status," which would entail an equal right to be spared suffering, as well as an equal right to life.[6] Also, she maintains that nonhumans need a number of legal rights in addition to the right not to be property.[7]

I agree. All sentient beings are entitled to equal moral consideration and equal legal protection from human abuse. Sentience is necessary and sufficient for rights. Nonhumans should share all legal rights currently reserved for humans that are relevant to their well-being. In the next chapter, I outline these rights.

To a nonspeciesist, it's morally acceptable to intentionally kill a nonhuman only under the same extraordinary circumstances under which it's morally acceptable to kill a human. One such circumstance is imminent starvation. In my view, you're morally entitled to kill and eat a nonhuman or human if no nutritionally adequate plant foods are available, you can't scavenge sufficient animal remains, and you've begun to die from malnutrition (a physician would diagnose you as starving).

Short of being stranded in a frozen wasteland or famine-stricken area devoid of plant food, no human is going to die because they avoid eating animal-derived food. If I'm starving in the Arctic and kill a polar bear in order to survive, haven't I violated the bear's right to life? No. I have an equal right to life. In such a situation, one individual's right to life competes with another's. If I have no other food source, I—like the polar bear—must kill prey if I want to survive. (Of course, the polar bear might kill *me* rather than the other way around.)

Isn't it speciesist for me to choose my life over the polar bear's? Again, no. In a crisis, we're entitled to choose either of two individuals (see chapter 5). I consider it acceptable to kill and eat a polar bear, a human, or anyone else to fend off otherwise-imminent starvation. I might not be *willing* to kill and eat someone, but I'd be morally entitled to.

Except that humans shouldn't interfere with predator–prey relationships among free-living nonhumans, I also think we're morally entitled to kill someone (as always, human or nonhuman) who directly, immediately threatens our life or that of another. I've been asked, "If a lion attacked your child or dog, wouldn't you wish that you could intervene?" I *would* intervene. I'd do everything in my power to defend my (hypothetical) child or dog. If necessary, I'd kill the lion. But I'd just as readily kill a *human* attacker.

I think we have a right to kill *anyone* who is invading our body or that of another (again, with the exception of natural situations among free-living nonhumans). For example, it's justifiable defense of self or another, such as a dog or cat, to kill parasites (unless they're external and can be removed benignly). Everyone has a right to bodily integrity. In keeping with U.S. law, I think an individual is entitled to kill an attacker if that's the only way to prevent being raped.

Genuine euthanasia—killing to end apparently incurable suffering—also is morally acceptable. Euthanasia includes suicide (self-euthanasia), assisted suicide, mercy killing of a human who wishes to die, and mercy killing of a nonhuman who quite clearly is experiencing incurable suffering. For example, if a cat or dog has stopped eating, barely moves, looks pained or depressed, and has been diagnosed with a terminal illness, euthanasia almost certainly is in their best interest.

Overall, however, the intentional killing of any sentient being is morally wrong. Except under extraordinary circumstances, humans have no moral right to intentionally deprive other animals of life, liberty, or well-being. Any needless harm to nonhumans should be viewed with the same disapproval as comparable harm to humans.

Sentient Beings

Are all animals sentient? By "sentient" I mean conscious, capable of experiencing thoughts or feelings. Who, exactly, should have rights?

As discussed in chapter 2, the scientific consensus is that all vertebrates are sentient. I see no good reason to doubt that they think and feel.

What about invertebrates? The vast majority of the world's living beings are invertebrates. Most animals are insects. Vastly more honeybees are exploited each year in the United States than all vertebrates combined, yet Francione excludes insects from "most of the animals we exploit."[8] He doesn't know whether insects are sentient, he says, but that "does not relieve me of my moral obligation to the animals whom I do know are sentient."[9] Our moral obligation needs to include insects and all other beings with a nervous system.

Although biologists currently classify them as animals, the following organisms lack a nervous system: sponges, rhombozoans (tiny worm-shaped parasites), orthonectids (microscopic worm-shaped parasites), and placozoans (which resemble amoebas but are multicellular). It's highly unlikely that these organisms—taxonomic anomalies—can experience pain or anything else. As I mentioned in the preface, because of their apparent insentience I don't include them in "animals." In my view, we needn't feel any concern for sponges, rhombozoans, orthonectids, or placozoans—not, at least, for their own sake.

All other organisms whom biologists currently classify as animals *do* have a nervous system. Therefore, we should assume that they can experience. (Biologists don't classify viruses, bacteria, or protoctists such as amoebas and paramecia as animals. Like plants, those organisms have no nervous system.)

All vertebrates and most invertebrates are bilaterally symmetrical (have a lengthwise body axis that divides them into left and right sides). Like all vertebrates, bilaterally symmetrical invertebrates possess a brain, defined as a primary nerve center in the head. Among others, these invertebrates include flatworms, earthworms, insects, mollusks, arachnids, and crustaceans.

Radial invertebrates, who radiate out from a center, don't have any apparent brain—at least, as traditionally defined—but do have a nervous system. These animals include comb jellies; cnidarians such as jellyfishes, hydras, sea anemones, and corals; and echinoderms such as sea urchins and sea stars (formerly called starfishes).

Invertebrate Pain

Francione comments that some animals who possess a nervous system may not be "capable of consciously experiencing pain and suffering."[10] Instead they may have only "nociceptive neural reactions" and "reflex" responses to tissue damage, with "no perception that it is the 'self' who is in pain."[11] It's unlikely that any animals have a nervous system that registers tissue damage yet lack awareness that the tissue being damaged is their own, and extremely improbable in the case of animals, such as insects, who possess a brain. Without some sense of "I," animals wouldn't learn to avoid whatever it was that caused the damage.

In chapter 2, I described humans who have congenital analgesia, a permanent inability to feel pain. Such a condition is highly maladaptive and anomalous in humans and probably similarly maladaptive and anomalous in other animals. Also, although they can't feel pain, humans with congenital analgesia have a sense of self. When they're burned, they're aware of heat. When a rock falls on their foot, they're aware of pressure. Heat and pressure just don't hurt. Humans who can't feel pain still are sentient: they experience a wide range of thoughts and feelings. Francione defines sentience as an ability to experience "pain" or "pain and suffering."[12] That definition is too narrow. Any conscious being is sentient.

In any case, abundant evidence indicates that all invertebrates with a brain can experience pain. Like vertebrates, numerous invertebrates produce natural opiates and substance P. These animals include crustaceans (e.g., crabs, lobsters, and shrimps), insects (e.g., fruit flies, locusts, and cockroaches), and mollusks (e.g., octopuses, squids, and snails).[13]

Also, crustaceans, insects, and mollusks show less reaction to a noxious stimulus when they receive morphine. For example, morphine reduces the reaction of mantis shrimps to electric shock, praying mantises to electric shock, and land snails to a hot surface.[14] (As I indicated earlier, I completely disapprove of vivisection, which I cite only to convince skeptics who place special stock in laboratory evidence.)

Crustaceans, insects, and mollusks learn to avoid a neutral, or even positive, stimulus associated with a noxious one. For instance, fruit flies will avoid particular odors, octopuses particular visual signals, and sea slugs particular foods associated with electric shock.[15] To learn such avoidance, animals must remember a negative experience—most likely, pain.

Crustaceans, insects, and mollusks *act* as if they experience pain. Dropped into boiling water, lobsters show struggling movements, not reflex reactions. Electrically shocked, marine snails pull in the part of their body that was shocked; release mucus, ink, and opaline; withdraw their gill and siphon; breathe more rapidly; and move away.[16] Poisoned with insecticides, insects writhe. Attacked, they produce sounds, alarm pheromones, and repellent secretions.[17] When a heated needle is brought close to their antennae, assassin bugs "react violently" and try to escape.[18] One of the world's foremost entomologists, Cambridge University professor V. B. Wigglesworth, has stated, "I am sure that insects can feel pain."[19]

Earthworms, flatworms (such as tapeworms), and leeches produce natural opiates.[20] When earthworms receive morphine, their efforts to escape aversive pressure are less intense.[21] Earthworms learn to avoid a taste associated with a hot, dry environment.[22] They writhe when impaled on a fishing hook. Flatworms learn to avoid foods and routes associated with electric shock.[23] Leeches learn to associate a light touch with electric shock: initially they crawl in response to a shock but not a touch; after a touch and shock have repeatedly been paired, a touch suffices to elicit crawling.[24] Stuck with a pin or pinched with a forceps, leeches coil or writhe.[25] Because of the evidence that worms can suffer, Bernard Rollin, who is a physiologist as well as an ethicist, includes worms among beings who have "interests."[26]

What about radial invertebrates, who lack a brain (as traditionally defined) but possess a nervous system? Hydras produce substance P.[27] Hydras, jellyfishes, and sea anemones show escape behaviors, such as withdrawing from harmful chemicals.[28]

Sea anemones are capable of associative learning apparently related to pain. For example, California shore anemones react to electric shock, but not bright light, by folding their tentacles and oral disk. After bright light has been paired with shock, the sea anemones react this way to the light alone—indicating that they've learned to associate the light with shock.[29]

There is strong evidence, then, that every animal with a brain can experience pain, as well as growing evidence that every animal with a nervous system can. All nervous systems have a shared ancestry and myriad physiological similarities. The capacity to feel pain confers survival advantages. Evolution would be inexplicably disjunct if only humans, only mammals, or only vertebrates could suffer.

Invertebrate Thought

Most humans assume that invertebrate brains are inferior to those of vertebrates. Individual nerve cells tend to be "more complex" in *invertebrate* brains.[30] Typically, vertebrate nerve cells project a single axon whereas invertebrate nerve cells branch out with several axons, each capable of independent action.

Also, invertebrates of numerous species possess a brain with many specialized regions. As a neurobiologist has remarked, the brains of crustaceans, insects, spiders, and other arthropods show "a high order of organizational complexity."[31] Octopuses have large, complex brains containing "vast numbers of interconnected neurons." Their "higher brain centers" appear to be, in many ways, "analogous to the cerebrum of higher vertebrates."[32]

Evidence of emotion and reasoning ability further indicates that invertebrates are conscious. Numerous researchers have commented on octopuses' intelligence, emotionality, and unique personalities. In nature, octopuses use stones to crack open mussels and to prop open the shells of large bivalves while eating their flesh.[33] Blinded octopuses distinguish between touching and *being* touched.[34] How could they do that without self-awareness?

Kept hungry and individually confined to small, nearly barren laboratory tanks, the common octopuses Albert, Bertram, and Charles learned to pull a lever for food. With each pull, they lit a lamp suspended just above the water and received part of a sardine. Whereas Albert and Bertram virtually ignored the lamp, Charles often yanked it underwater. Floating in place, Albert and Bertram moved the lever gently. Latching onto the tank's side with several tentacles and grasping the lever with others, Charles "applied great force" until, after ten days of repeated bending, the lever broke. Of the three octopuses, only Charles habitually waited, eyes just above the water's surface, for a human to approach and then squirted them with water.[35] The three octopuses experienced nearly identical environments, but Charles behaved in a markedly singular way. He differed from Albert and Bertram in temperament.

Mantis shrimps can recognize individuals of their species by smell. When seeking a shelter, they avoid an empty cavity that contains the odor of a mantis shrimp who previously defeated them in a competitive encounter but enter a cavity that contains the odor of a mantis shrimp whom *they* previously defeated.[36] They learn and remember.

Boxer crabs use sea anemones' stinging tentacles as weapons. The crabs detach anemones from rocks, keep one in each claw, "maintain" the anemones by removing particles that cling to their surface, and "replace" the anemones if they fragment. When threatened, the crabs turn toward their possible attacker and wave the anemones, who sting any animal who comes too close.[37]

"The traditional view of the insect brain as limited and inflexible, compared with the vertebrate brain, has given way over the past several decades as research continually reveals unsuspected degrees of sophistication," neuroscientists Bruno van Swinderen and Ralph Greenspan comment.[38]

Having found food, honeybee workers return to their hive and communicate its location to their sisters. Using a symbolic system, they dance a message of direction and distance that varies with the time of day and a food source's unique location. As reported in chapter 6, honeybees show much other behavior that indicates reasoning. "Honeybees are capable of such complex cognitive functions as associative recall, categorization, contextual learning, allocentric navigational memory [independent of one's own spatial position], and certain forms of abstraction," van Swinderen and Greenspan note.[39]

In the words of two other cognitive scientists, "Fruit flies can learn a lot of things." For example, they "run away from specific odors that they previously experienced with electric shock" and "run toward odors previously associated with sugar." Like humans, flies have both short-term and long-term memory.[40]

Naturalists have observed the following wasp actions. Finding caterpillar prey too heavy for takeoff, a wasp split the body in two, flew off with one half, and soon returned for the rest.[41] After catching a fly nearly her own size, another wasp lightened her load by detaching her prey's abdomen and head. Grasping the remaining thorax, she attempted flight. A breeze caught the wings still attached to the fly's thorax and blew the wasp about. She landed, bit off the impediments, and flew away with the streamlined body part.[42] Unable to take flight while holding a grasshopper's body several times her own size, a third wasp dragged the body about 30 feet to a tree, carried it to the top, and leaped off into flight.[43]

Instinct can't account for the flexibility and variability of wasp behavior. Faced with different problems, three wasps found different, efficient solutions. Their behavior indicates insight and a capacity to learn from experience, such as the experience that it's easier to remain airborne after leaping from a height than it is to become airborne via liftoff. A stimulus–response explanation would be forced, requiring an elaborate, serendipitous combination of preprogrammed reactions. Problem-solving ability has survival value for wasps as well as humans.

After depositing an egg in an underground burrow, a digger wasp seals the entrance by wedging a pebble into it or filling it with soil that she tamps down with a pebble, piece of bark, or other small object held in her jaws.[44] A female sand wasp prepares a chamber for her offspring by digging into a sand dune and plugging the hole. She then flies away and obtains prey: a paralyzed caterpillar. She returns with the caterpillar, unplugs the chamber, pushes the caterpillar inside, deposits an egg, and reseals the chamber. When the egg hatches, the larva starts to eat the caterpillar. Every morning, the mother returns to the chamber and, as expressed by two zoologists, "assesses" the size of both the larva and the caterpillar. When the caterpillar is nearly gone, she brings another. A sand-wasp mother usually tends two or three larvae during the same period, in different locations. Using landmarks, she remembers the location of each concealed chamber. She also remembers which larva needs additional food.[45]

Similarly to digger and sand wasps, a beetle was observed to dig a hole in peat and insert a caterpillar. There being no pebbles nearby, the beetle flew away, returned with a pebble, and placed it over the hole before flying off.[46]

To attract termite prey, assassin bugs dangle termite remains over a hole in a termite nest. When a termite attempts to pull the edible remains into the nest, the assassin bug grabs and kills the termite.[47]

Many people have reported seeing ants construct a bridge over water or some other barrier—for example, by taking shreds of grass and, using their saliva, gluing them together.[48] Ants of various species use bits of leaf, wood, dirt, or sand as food-collecting tools. Holding such material in their jaws, they dip it into food (e.g., honey, fruit pulp, or the body fluids of prey) until the food sticks or is absorbed. Then they carry the soaked material back to their colony. This strategy substantially increases the amount of food that they can carry.[49] Why do humans consider it intelligence when chimpanzees use leaves as sponges to absorb water, or woodpeckers soak bark in honey that they then feed to their young, but mere instinct when ants perform equally complex actions? Speciesism.

An eyewitness reported the following behavior of a garden spider. After a storm destroyed her web's bottom connecting strands, the spider descended to the ground by a thread, crawled over to some wood fragments, brought one back to her web, and hung it from the bottom. With the wood acting as an anchor, her web survived the storm. When good weather returned, the spider mended her web and broke the thread holding the wood, letting the now-useless aid fall to the ground.[50] Another eyewitness report tells of a spider who used a stone to secure her web.[51]

Hunting spiders build rafts by rolling leaves into "logs" that they tie, and then bind together, with sticky thread exuded from their body. The spiders float on the rafts to catch water insects.[52]

Jumping spiders of the genus *Portia* frequently enter the webs of other spiders, on whom they prey. Because web-building spiders are extremely sensitive to web tension and vibration but have poor vision, *Portia* spiders exploit and manipulate web vibration in order to disguise their presence within another spider's web. Sometimes they advance across the web while either the wind or the struggles of an insect caught in the web are creating vibratory "background noise." At other times, they vibrate the web in a way that mimics such background noise. *Portia* spiders may try different vibration patterns until one causes the prey to approach, in which case they then continue using that pattern for that particular prey.[53]

Portia spiders also use a detour strategy that enables them to attack a spider without first entering that spider's web. For example, *Portia* spiders have been seen taking the following steps to capture spiders whose webs are beneath vegetation. First the *Portia* spider observes the web and its surrounding vegetation (*Portia* spiders have excellent vision). Next they move away from the prey. The detour may last for hours, during which the prey may be out of view for extended periods. Then the *Portia* spider approaches the prey's web so as to arrive at the overhanging vegetation. From there they drop down, by means of their body thread, to a position alongside the other spider, without touching the web. Finally they swing in to kill the other spider.[54]

"After recognizing prey for which an indirect approach is appropriate, *Portia* apparently plans a solution to the problem of how to reach the prey along a path over terrain never crossed before," say the researchers who observed *Portia* spiders' strategizing.[55] "It is difficult to escape the conclusion that *Portia* solves detour problems in its head, makes plans, and then acts on these plans."[56] *Portia* spiders use different strategies, including deception, for different situations. They make a mental map of their environment. They imagine what they're going to do before they do it. Where does anyone imagine anything? In their mind. Spiders have a mind. "It would be contrived to deny at least the rudiments of cognition in *Portia*," the researchers comment.[57]

Radial invertebrates, too, show consciousness. Giant sea stars normally eat mussels and barnacles. In an experiment, giant sea stars ordinarily stayed high on the walls of their individual tanks. In the experiment's first phase, a light periodically would come on for 15 minutes. The sea stars would remain near the top of their tank. In the experiment's second phase, the light would come on at the same time that a mussel was placed on the bottom of their tank. The sea stars would quickly move down to seize the mussel. In the third phase, the light would come on 15 minutes before a mussel was provided. The sea stars would move down more slowly than in the previous phase and wait, at the bottom of their tank, for a mussel. In the final phase, the light would come on, but the sea stars wouldn't receive any food. They soon stopped moving down in response to the light. The sea stars discerned an association between light and a mussel, as well as that association's end. Sea stars "learn," the experimenter states. He warns against the assumption that radial shape or an apparently simple nervous system means little or no learning capacity. Multiple studies indicate that a sea star's nerve ring acts as a control center—that is, like a brain.[58]

There's no good reason to lack confidence that animals who possess a brain are sentient. All such animals should receive equal consideration. Am I saying that a firefly is as fully entitled to moral consideration as a rabbit or bonobo? Yes. Am I saying that a spider has as much right to life as an egret or human? Yes. I see no logically consistent reason to say otherwise.

Evidence and evolutionary theory also indicate that animals who possess a nervous system but no apparent brain are sentient. Therefore, they too should receive moral consideration and basic legal rights.

Sentience, defined as any capacity to experience, is the only logical and fair basis for rights. In nonspeciesist philosophy, all sentient beings have rights. What's more, all sentient beings are equal.

9

Nonspeciesist Law

The law should protect the innocent and penalize the guilty, most humans would agree. Inbreeding, confinement, beatings, and other human abuses can make nonhumans aggressive. Otherwise, few nonhumans seriously injure or kill except out of immediate necessity. Unless abused, most nonhumans cause serious harm only to preserve themselves or others. Nonhumans who do inflict apparently gratuitous harm may have no sense of wrongdoing. As with young children and mentally incompetent adults, we shouldn't hold them accountable. By the legal standards of human democratic societies, nonhumans are innocent. Yet, the law fails to protect them.

When we cause no more harm than we must to survive, we too are innocent. We're innocent when we sustain ourselves by growing crops for human consumption. Inadvertently, nonhumans will be hurt or killed, but far fewer than in "animal agriculture," which entails feeding crops to nonhumans who are intentionally killed. We're innocent when we hurt or kill someone who directly threatens us or another. It isn't wrong to kill a tiger who leaps at our throat or a tapeworm who invades a dog's body.

It *is* wrong to harm nonhumans for information and career advancement (vivisection); entertainment (sport fishing, hunting, aquaprisons...); pet-keeping (human breeding of dogs and cats, trafficking in exotic pets...); vanity (pearls, silk, nonhuman hair and skin...); culinary habit, preference, or convenience (honey, flesh, eggs...); profit (all of the above); or any other reason beyond immediate, direct necessity. We're guilty if we knowingly participate in needless, unjust practices that cause suffering or death. Most humans are guilty. Yet, the law fails to penalize them.

Present law serves speciesism rather than justice. The owner of a single egg factory causes millions of hens to live in relentless physical and psychological pain and die from deprivation, disease, or murder. Instead of charging such a person with atrocities, society rewards them with money and respectability. From trappers to vivisectors, humans guilty of torturing, enslaving, and murdering nonhumans retain freedom and life while their innocent victims do not.

With regard to humans, democratic law honors individuals' fundamental rights, which can't be discarded for others' benefit. Utilitarian calculations such as cost-benefit analyses come into play only within a context that respects those rights. Nonhumans, too, should have legal rights invulnerable to utilitarian considerations.

Emancipation

In *The Case for Animal Rights*, Tom Regan made this groundbreaking statement: "The rights view challenges the very conception of animals as legal property."[1] Logic and evidence compel us to reject nonhumans' current property status as unjust.

In various eras and cultures, the law has classified women, children, or humans of other categories as property. Today human slavery is illegal worldwide. We consider it immoral to treat any human, whatever their characteristics, as property. It's equally immoral to treat any nonhuman as property. Currently, though, nonhuman slavery is universal.

As you'll recall, the U.S. Constitution's 13th Amendment (1865) states, "Neither slavery nor involuntary servitude, except as a punishment for crime whereof the party shall have been duly convicted, shall exist within the United States, or any place subject to their jurisdiction." Slavery, you'll notice, needn't involve involuntary labor; anyone held as property is enslaved.

The amendment's effect was to emancipate enslaved African-Americans. Its promise, however, awaits fulfillment. Because the amendment is interpreted as prohibiting only human slavery, nonhuman slavery continues to exist within the United States on a massive scale.

The vast majority of Americans have a vested interest in preserving nonhuman enslavement. The only Americans who seek slavery's abolition—animal rights advocates—constitute a small minority.

The U.S. government is deeply involved in nonhuman exploitation. The Department of Agriculture subsidizes and promotes the flesh, egg, honey, and milk industries. The National Institutes of Health fund vivisection. The Food and Drug Administration requires that drugs be tested on nonhumans. The Department of Defense uses dolphins, dogs, and other nonhumans for military purposes. The Fish and Wildlife Service supports hunting, fishing, and trapping. And on and on.

State and local governments, too, have strong ties to nonhuman exploitation. They fund and otherwise support such abuses as fishing, hunting, dissection, vivisection, aquaprisons, zoos, "aquaculture," and "animal agriculture."

How, then, could some or all nonhumans be emancipated?

The Constitution doesn't define *person*. As discussed in chapter 6, *person*'s legal meaning has expanded over time. Congress could pass a constitutional amendment declaring some or all nonhumans to be persons under the Constitution, rather than property. The 13th Amendment then would apply to those nonhumans.

However, a constitutional amendment requires broad public support. Members of Congress are beholden to their constituents and financial contributors. Also, at least three-fourths (38) of the 50 state legislatures must ratify a constitutional amendment. Therefore, no amendment emancipating most or all nonhumans will be possible until many more Americans reject animal-derived products and endorse nonhuman rights.

Alternatively to emancipation first being legislated by Congress, it could first be mandated by the Supreme Court. In *Minneapolis & St. Louis Railroad v. Beckwith* (1889) and *Noble v. Union River Logging* (1893), the Supreme Court ruled that a corporation is a "person" for the purposes of due process and equal protection under Amendments 14 (1868) and 5 (1791), respectively. The Court similarly could rule that some or all nonhumans are constitutional persons.

Almost certainly, the first cases for nonhuman emancipation would seek personhood for nonhumans of one or more particular species, such as chimpanzees or dolphins. Such cases would begin in lower courts and, through a series of appeals, proceed to higher ones.

Eventually they would reach the Supreme Court, which could rule that the animals in question aren't properly regarded as human property but should be legal persons.[2]

Over time, the Supreme Court could rule that all sentient beings should be free: persons under the Constitution. The precedents for such a ruling would include all successful sentience-based cases for particular species, as well as cases (such as *Superintendent of Belchertown v. Saikewicz* and *Youngberg v. Romeo*) in which judges have asserted the rights of humans who are sentient but lack intelligence of the kind typically associated with humans.[3]

The end of legal slavery would free nonhumans from human ownership. Slave laws such as the Animal Welfare Act, the Humane Methods of Slaughter Act, and state cruelty statutes would become void.

Ex-slaveholders would not be compensated for the loss of their former property. When enslaved African-Americans were emancipated, their former owners received no compensation. Nor should nonhumans' former owners be compensated. The Fifth Amendment prohibits the federal government from taking private property for public use "without just compensation." However, nonhumans no longer would be property, the government wouldn't be taking them for public use, and compensating ex-slaveholders wouldn't be just. Nonhumans never were rightfully human property. Captive nonhumans are kidnapped individuals or descendants of such individuals. To the fullest extent possible, compensation should go to slavery's victims, not its perpetrators.

All captive nonhumans would be liberated from exploitation and abusive confinement. Those experiencing apparently incurable suffering would be euthanized; all others would receive any needed veterinary care. Remember: by this time, far fewer nonhumans would be captive than today; a much larger percentage of the public already would be vegans, who reject products of nonhuman exploitation. The end of nonhuman enslavement would liberate elephants from circuses, hens from egg factories, and rats from vivisection laboratories (unless these animals already were free; most likely, elephants will be emancipated before chickens or rats).

Turkeys freed from flesh factories, cats freed from "shelters," and other homeless "domesticated" nonhumans would be fostered at sanctuaries and private homes until adopted. A screening process would help to safeguard each adoptee's well-being. Nonhumans in human care would have essentially the same legal rights as young children.[4]

A ban on human breeding of nonhumans would end thousands of years of inflicting deformity and genetic disease. The "production" of nonhumans for vivisection, slaughter, and any other purpose (including pet-keeping) would cease. The number of "domesticated" nonhumans would rapidly decline.

Non-"domesticated" captives would be set free if they could thrive without human assistance (after any necessary rehabilitation) and if appropriate habitat existed. If not, they would be permanently cared for at sanctuaries. As much as possible, these sanctuaries would provide natural, fulfilling environments.

All Applicable Rights

In addition to emancipating nonhumans, constitutional personhood would give them personhood throughout federal and state law.

Gary Francione states, "We are obligated to extend to animals [sic] only *one* right—the right not to be treated as the property of humans."[5] I disagree. Freedom from enslavement (property status) is the prerequisite for legal rights. In Paola Cavalieri's words, property status is "the basic obstacle" to nonhuman rights; freeing nonhumans from that status is the point of departure, not arrival.[6] With regard to humans, Francione calls the right not to be treated as property the "grounding" for other rights.[7] In my view, the same applies to nonhumans.

Francione doesn't advocate that nonhumans have "the same legal rights (constitutional or otherwise) that we accord humans."[8] I advocate that nonhumans have all such rights that are applicable. In the United States, constitutional personhood seems the most likely means of nonhuman emancipation. In fact, I'm not aware of any way, within the current U.S. legal system, that nonhumans could be freed from property status *without* becoming constitutional persons. If nonhumans were constitutional persons, constitutional rights would flow to them as a matter of course.

Many constitutional rights aren't relevant to nonhumans. Other animals can't use a right to trial by jury or freedom of religion. (They're too rational for religion.) In the 1980s a Georgia couple bought a business license allowing them to solicit money, from Augusta pedestrians, for "speech" (such as "I love you") by their cat Blackie. The couple filed suit on the grounds that a business-license requirement violated Blackie's First Amendment rights to freedom of speech and association. Not surprisingly, the court ruled that cats aren't constitutional persons and therefore have no such rights.[9] This case parodies what animal rights advocates seek. We don't seek freedom of speech for cats and other nonhumans. We want exploitive, ownership-based situations such as Blackie's to end.

Amendments 5 and 14 bestow the constitutional rights most applicable to nonhumans. The Fifth Amendment applies to the federal government and the District of Columbia; the 14th applies to state governments. These amendments prohibit government from depriving any "person" of "life, liberty, or property, without due process of law."

"Liberty" includes bodily integrity and physical freedom. If nonhumans were constitutional persons, governments couldn't subject them to maiming, battery, torture, or other bodily harm. Nor could governments unjustly incarcerate them or otherwise restrict their movements.

"Without due process of law" means unfairly or arbitrarily. The Constitution prohibits government from depriving a "person" of life, liberty, or property for patently unjust reasons or without following proper judicial procedure. Nonhuman personhood would prohibit government from unjustifiably depriving nonhumans of life, liberty, or property.

As interpreted by the courts, the Fifth Amendment also requires that constitutional persons receive equal protection under federal laws: comparable treatment in comparable situations. If nonhumans were constitutional persons, their basic interests would command the same respect under federal law as comparable human interests. Nonhumans would be persons under federal statutes, compiled in the U.S. Code.

In addition to providing some protections against government, federal statutes provide various protections against nongovernmental individuals and organizations (including companies). They prohibit a

number of abuses—such as interstate kidnapping and maritime murder—highly relevant to nonhumans. Like young children and mentally incompetent human adults, nonhumans would be protected, but
not accountable, under the U.S. Code.

The U.S. Code's opening section (the Dictionary Act) defines
person as used throughout the Code. In 1874 Congress expanded the
Code's definition of *person* to include corporations. If nonhumans
were accorded constitutional personhood, this definition would en-
compass them as well.

The 14th Amendment expressly grants constitutional persons
"equal protection" under state laws. State laws provide "persons"
with a number of basic protections that nonhumans also need. For
example, state laws prohibit murdering, battering, sexually assault-
ing, or stealing from a "person." As constitutional persons, nonhumans would be persons under state laws (again, without accountability).

Nonhumans need a number of the rights that constitutional personhood confers on humans, such as a right to life. Eventually after
emancipation, virtually all nonhumans would be free-living and non-
"domesticated." Free-living nonhumans can't be completely isolated
from humans. Geese visit "our" ponds; squirrels enter our backyards;
pigeons roost on our buildings. We encounter bears in the forest and
crabs on the seashore. Wherever they may be, nonhumans need protection against humans. They need legal rights that prevent human
interference. Unless buzzards and coyotes have a legal right to life,
humans can shoot or poison them with impunity.

Following emancipation, humans couldn't legally hunt, Francione
says, because hunting is "a form of institutionalized exploitation."[10]
In its current form, yes. However, individual humans could hunt unless emancipated nonhumans had a legal right to life.

Francione sometimes refers to the "one right" that he advocates
for nonhumans as the right "not to be treated as a resource."[11] If I
murder a human out of anger, I haven't treated them as a resource.
Nevertheless, I've violated their right to life. Nonhuman rights, too,
can be violated whether or not nonhumans are regarded as resources.
When an exterminator murders all of the wasps who live in a nest
attached to a house, the wasps are viewed as pests, not resources.
Their murder doesn't involve any exploitation. Wasps need a legal
right to life. Similarly, when humans kill a nonpoisonous snake out

of irrational fear and dislike, they aren't treating the snake as a resource. Snakes need a legal right to life.

According to Francione, abolishing institutionalized speciesist
exploitation would eliminate the vast majority of human–nonhuman
conflicts.[12] I agree that emancipation would eliminate a massive
amount of nonhuman suffering and death. However, it wouldn't
eliminate nonhuman–human conflicts over land or other natural resources such as water. These conflicts are ongoing and worldwide.

Routinely, humans simply kill their nonhuman "competitors."
They readily exterminate insects, rodents, and other small animals
even when benign measures, such as improved sanitation, would re-
solve any serious conflicts. Such killing involves no exploitation.

Francione advocates "equal consideration" for all sentient beings.[13] Surely, equal consideration entails much more than not treating nonhumans as resources.

Along with a legal right to life, emancipated nonhumans would
need a legal right to liberty (which includes physical freedom and
bodily integrity). Without such a right, they could be trapped, confined, and otherwise denied physical freedom by any human who
considered them a nuisance or threat.

Without a right to liberty, nonhumans also would be vulnerable to
human violations of their bodily integrity. Consider "domesticated"
sheep who would exist during the transition period immediately
following emancipation. No longer property, they still would need
legal protection against battery or sexual assault by a human, just as
humans do. Similarly, a right not to be tortured exists apart from a
right not to be property. Although property status vastly increases the
opportunity for sadism, it isn't a necessary component of sadism. A
human can torture a dog whether or not the dog is property.

Amendments 5 and 14 also specify a right to one's property.
Should nonhumans have such a right? In my view, yes.

Just as humans have no moral right to treat nonhumans as human
property, they have no right to treat what, in fairness, belongs to
nonhumans as human property. Nonhumans should be regarded as
owning what they produce (eggs, milk, honey, pearls...), what they
build (nests, bowers, hives...), and the natural habitats in which they
live (marshlands, forests, lakes, oceans...).

As much as a woman, a cow has a moral right to milk that she
produces. Free to choose, she would give this milk to her calf, not to

humans. The law should regard the milk of a cow, or any other animal, as that individual's personal property. Similarly, bees have a moral right to the honey that they produce to nourish colony members. The law should regard honey as the colony's communal property. Legally, nonhumans should own the products of their bodies and labors.

Most likely, emancipation would end most human theft of these products. However, without a nonhuman right to property, humans still would feel free to take from nonhumans—for example, take honey from a beehive or eggs from a robin nest. They'd also feel free to destroy nonhuman creations, such as a beehive or nest. A structure built by nonhumans should legally belong to its creators and their descendents. Consider a dam built by beavers. Its destruction can mean suffering and death for the beavers as well as many other animals within the ecosystem that has developed around the dam.

With the possible exception of the right not to be murdered by humans, the most important right for free nonhumans probably is the right to their habitats. Steve Sapontzis has voiced the possibility of expanding our concept of property to include nonhuman territory.[14] I think we need to do this.

All nonhumans living in a particular area of land or water should have a legal right to that environment, which should be considered their communal property. The law should prohibit humans from appropriating or intentionally harming that property. Nonhuman territory should be off-limits to further human encroachment.

Currently, humans regularly drain ponds, bulldoze woodlands, and otherwise destroy nonhuman habitat. This destruction causes incalculable suffering and death. After nonhuman emancipation, humans could continue to destroy nonhuman habitat unless legally prohibited.

Humans still would want to build homes in "areas now occupied exclusively by nonhumans," Francione notes.[15] He doesn't advocate a nonhuman right to territory (or any other property).[16] How, then, does he propose that we handle human–nonhuman territory conflicts? We should "try" to give the nonhumans equal consideration, make at least "a good-faith effort" not to intentionally kill them, and, if necessary, "relocate" them.[17] "Try" to give them equal consideration? As Francione himself emphasizes, equal consideration is the foundational principle of justice toward nonhumans: "imperative."[18] Applying that principle is the first step to finding the most equitable solution to any conflict. Make an "effort" not to kill them? We should intentionally kill nonhumans only under extraordinary circumstances, such as those requiring immediate self-defense (see the previous chapter). "Relocate" them? Why should nonhumans make way for further human sprawl?

Francione refers to "deer overpopulation."[19] Deer aren't overpopulated. When humans don't interfere with deer or their territory, deer populations adjust to their ecosystem's available resources. Humans need to reduce their own population size. Nonhumans have a moral right to their home territory.

Outside a context of exploitation, Francione allows human interests to trump nonhuman ones. In his view all sentient beings have a right not to be human property, but they don't all have "the same value for purposes of resolving conflicts between rightholders."[20] That is, nonhuman rights-holders won't necessarily have the same value as humans. When conflicts arise between humans and free nonhumans, he says, "it may be *permissible*" to consider whether the nonhumans possess particular "virtues" (such as a certain level of human-like intelligence).[21]

As Cavalieri comments, equal consideration means that *all* members of the moral community have equal value and that equivalent claims are accorded equal weight.[22] Equality requires that individuals, whatever their traits, receive comparable treatment.[23] Francione gives nonhuman claims less weight than equivalent, and even lesser, human claims. Like Peter Singer and Tom Regan, he indicates that the lack of some trait can count against nonhumans: "empirical differences between humans and nonhumans" might justify their "differential treatment."[24]

Francione gives an example of the sort of differential treatment that he finds acceptable: we might decide that "developers" are morally entitled to displace field mice, but not humans, from their current homes. Francione rationalizes our "moving the mice from one field to another": we might "determine (as best we can)" that mice care less about their home territory than humans care about that territory.[25] It's much easier for humans to appreciate human needs and desires than nonhuman ones, so they shouldn't presume to judge how much field mice value their habitat. Also, the extent to which mice consciously value their habitat doesn't equate to how much they *need* that habitat.

Francione is doing something to which he strenuously objects throughout his work: he's "balancing" interests using scales already weighted on one side. As he repeatedly notes, when the interests of rights-holders (humans) are "balanced" against those of non-rights-holders (nonhumans), the rights-holders always win.[26] Similarly, if the interests of property-holders (humans) are balanced against those of non-property-holders (free nonhumans), the property-holders always will win. If humans have property rights but field mice don't, humans will win any territory conflicts.

Field mice build homes such as nests and extensive multi-chamber burrows. Often these homes are used by successive generations. However invisible to us, field-mouse homes have importance to their residents. It's self-serving to rationalize that humans are entitled to take and "develop" nonhuman land because they'll better appreciate and use that land. Whites offered the same self-justification for taking and "developing" Native American land. Like Native Americans, the field mice were there first. They're the rightful property-holders. Enslavement is wrong, but so is forced displacement.

Further, forcibly removing nonhumans from their homes violates rights other than their right to property. Trapping and transport temporarily deprive nonhumans of liberty. In contrast, prohibiting humans from building on land currently inhabited only by nonhumans doesn't violate humans' right to physical freedom.

Nonhumans live in a particular place because they've chosen to go or remain there. Removing them deprives them of autonomy. We have no right to choose for them (actually, for ourselves). Nonhumans have a right to noninterference from humans. In fact, that's the essence of nonhuman rights.

Humans can live in good health without new housing complexes. (In addition to reducing their reproduction, humans can replace single-family houses with high-rises, thereby housing many more humans on the same amount of land.) In contrast, the very survival of nonhumans may depend on their remaining in their habitat. For all we know, a particular field contains something crucial to field mice that another field lacks.

Francione suggests that field mice can be harmlessly trapped and dropped off at another field. That field, too, will already be inhabited. When nonhumans must compete for resources, conflicts among them increase. Many nonhumans will fiercely defend their territory from newcomers. Displacing nonhumans is unfair both to the displaced animals and to those whose territory they enter. Especially if resources prove inadequate, the result can be considerable suffering and death.

Even if nonhumans were displaced by new housing without being bodily removed, construction could be expected to destroy many of their homes, reduce their food sources, disrupt their communities, and force at least some of them into other territory. When it comes to "undeveloped" habitat, nonhuman interests seem much more vital than human ones.

Bernard Rollin has argued that converting undeveloped acreage into a golf course would serve the "inessential interests of a few" while harming the important interests of many, by destroying "thousands of sentient creatures' habitats."[27] A golf course is more frivolous than a new housing complex, but Rollin's point applies to both: nonhumans shouldn't be displaced for the sake of far fewer humans, especially when the nonhumans have more-vital interests at stake.

In sum, if nonhumans really receive equal consideration, "undeveloped" habitat must remain theirs. Land currently inhabited by nonhumans and humans can remain cohabited, but humans shouldn't be permitted to encroach farther into nonhuman territory (for example, by building yet-more housing developments on land occupied only by nonhumans). If humans don't want to be more crowded in already-"developed" areas, they can practice zero population growth.

Environmentalists are rightly concerned about habitat destruction and species extinctions. A nonhuman right to territory would greatly combat those problems.

I believe that making nonhuman habitat off-limits to human "development" (and other harm) would benefit humans as well as nonhumans. If the human population keeps increasing and we keep destroying natural habitat, the Earth will be inhospitable to nonhumans *and* humans. However, even if a hands-off policy toward nonhuman habitat didn't benefit humans, fairness would require such a policy. The Earth belongs to all of its inhabitants.

Nonhumans, of course, never would know that humans had given them a legal right to their home territory. Humans are the only ones who need to know. They need to know that their ownership doesn't extend to nonhumans, what nonhumans produce and create, *or* their habitats.

Cavalieri's book *The Animal Question* is subtitled *Why Nonhuman Animals Deserve Human Rights*. Nonhumans should have every relevant legal right currently reserved for humans, such as a right not to be kidnapped, maimed, or murdered. Emancipated nonhumans wouldn't be integrated into human society; nonhumans' forced "participation" in human society would end. However, free and independent nonhumans would need legal protection from humans. Racism toward African-Americans didn't end when they ceased to be property. Nor will speciesism end when nonhumans cease to be property. Free humans have legal rights. Free nonhumans must have them as well.

Equality

As legal persons, nonhumans would have legal standing. Humans could initiate criminal proceedings on their behalf, bring civil lawsuits on their behalf, and represent their interests in court. Law officers would be obligated to charge a fisher with torture or murder, block a building project that would destroy nonhuman habitat, or, during the transition period following emancipation, remove monkeys from an unfit "sanctuary." Nonhuman-rights advocates, police officers, prosecutors, judges, and others would act to prevent, halt, and (as much as possible) redress human harm to nonhumans.

Francione poses this question: Would nonhuman rights require that a human who kills a nonhuman be punished as they would be if the victim were human? He answers, "Of course not." According moral value to nonhumans doesn't require that a human who wrongfully harms a nonhuman receive the same penalty as one who harms a human in the same way and circumstances, he notes.[28] In my view, according *equal* moral value to nonhumans does require that comparable harm to humans and nonhumans carry equivalent penalty. Like human equality, animal equality doesn't mean much if it doesn't include equality under the law. Nonhumans should share, in full, all applicable protections that the law affords to humans.

Granting legal rights to nonhumans means placing new restrictions on humans. This is true of every expansion of human rights as well. For example, emancipating African-Americans meant prohibiting U.S. residents from holding other humans as property. We cherish our legal rights, which others may violate only at their peril. Our rights limit what others may do to us. Nonhumans deserve equal protection.

It should be illegal for any human to

buy, sell, breed, exhibit, imprison, deprive, or torture any nonhuman being;

use any nonhuman being in an experiment not undertaken for that individual's own potential benefit;

compel any nonhuman being to labor, perform, compete, or provide any service to humans;

intentionally kill any nonhuman being except to end their apparently incurable suffering; prevent them from parasitizing, injuring, or killing someone; or prevent someone's imminent starvation;

intentionally injure any nonhuman being except in someone's defense;

interfere with normal predation or other natural activities among free-living nonhumans;

take, intentionally damage, or intentionally destroy anything that nonhumans produce or create within their natural habitats;

intentionally destroy or dramatically alter any "undeveloped" habitat.

The rationale for legal rights is to minimize injustice and compensate its victims. Ideally, moral and legal rights would fully corre-

spond. All sentient beings have moral rights. They need corresponding legal rights.

When the law becomes nonspeciesist, all sentient beings will be persons throughout the law. All applicable legal protections currently
accorded to humans will be extended to other animals. This doesn't
mean that nonhumans will participate in human society. To the contrary, they'll be liberated from human society and other human interference.

Before the law can change in such a far-reaching way, public
opinion must change. Many more people must recognize and reject
speciesism.

10

Nonspeciesist Advocacy

In contrast to old-speciesist and new-speciesist advocacy, nonspeciesist advocacy advances the goal of emancipating all sentient beings from human abuse. It moves society closer to the view that all forms of speciesist exploitation—from dog breeding to commercial fishing—are morally wrong. The most effective animal rights advocacy erodes speciesism, exposing its falsehood and injustice.

Advocates for animal equality can reduce the abuse and murder of nonhumans while advancing total liberation. But that requires a nonspeciesist approach. Advocates shouldn't participate, either directly or indirectly, in any practice that violates nonhumans' moral rights. Nor should they suggest that it's acceptable to violate those rights. They should show zero tolerance of speciesist abuse.

Rescue

One way to reduce the number of abused and killed nonhumans is, of course, direct rescue. Adoption prevents a cat from being killed in a "shelter" or a rat from being killed after use in a school "science" project. Liberation saves a hen from further suffering, and then death, within the egg industry. In addition to rescuing one or a few individuals, activists can maintain sanctuaries for dozens or more nonhumans.

Such actions are nonspeciesist, akin to saving individual Jews from the Holocaust or helping individual African-Americans escape from slavery. Providing sanctuary to those in need in no way violates their rights. It gets them out of danger and frees them from abuse.

Unfortunately, direct rescue can save relatively few nonhumans.

Also, in many cases, exploiters quickly "replace" rescued animals. For example, vivisectors readily buy new animals to use in experimentation interrupted by rescue; they start over with new victims.

Abolitionist Bans

Another way to get nonhumans out of abusive situations is through abolitionist bans. As discussed in chapter 4, many activists misunderstand the term *abolitionist*. Bans aren't automatically abolitionist. Yes, a ban abolishes something. However, if it leaves the animals in question within a situation of exploitation (such as food-industry enslavement and slaughter), it isn't abolitionist in the sense of being anti-slavery. An abolitionist ban is consistent with nonhuman freedom. It prevents or halts, rather than mitigates, abuse.

All abolitionist bans protect at least some animals from some form of exploitation. They prevent animals from entering the situation of exploitation and may also remove current victims from that situation. Consider a ban on elephants in "animal acts." Abolitionist? Yes. Such a ban doesn't necessarily emancipate all elephants within a particular jurisdiction; for example, it doesn't prevent elephants from being exploited in zoos. However, it *does* prevent their being exploited in circuses and other performance situations. More than a dozen U.S. cities already have banned "animal acts" with elephants and other "wild" animals.

A ban on nonhuman primates in vivisection also is abolitionist. Although it doesn't free nonhuman primates from zoos or "animal acts," it does free them from vivisection.

A ban on bear hunting? Abolitionist. It prevents bears from being wounded or killed by hunters—prevents, rather than modifies, their abuse. Such a ban doesn't state, "Bears are persons, not property," but it's *consistent with* their not being property.

Abolitionist bans respect the moral rights of the nonhumans they're intended to protect. They're analogous to laws prohibiting child labor. Such laws didn't modify the treatment of children forced to labor. They prohibited the exploitation itself.

Many activists regard "welfarist" changes as quicker than abolitionist bans. Abolitionist bans—for instance, on cockfighting or leghold traps—can be enacted and implemented just as quickly as "welfarist" legislation, often more quickly.

Unfortunately, human abuse of nonhumans is so massive and diverse that there's no lack of abolitionist bans for which activists can campaign. Among numerous others, these include bans on exotic pets, rodeo, the calf-flesh industry, seal hunting, "fur farming," wolf killing, greyhound racing, dog breeding, and cosmetics testing on nonhumans.

Some readers might think, "OK, but the vast majority of exploited nonhumans are exploited for food. The bans you mention address the plight of comparatively few animals." Abolitionist bans on U.S. horse slaughter and "foie gras" production could be won in the near future, ending the U.S. horse-flesh and fatty-bird-liver industries. It's true, however, that outlawing a major food industry is virtually impossible. We can't ban the egg, cow-milk, or pig-flesh industry until many more people reject those industries' products. For now, the best way to combat massive industries based on speciesist abuse is to promote veganism and build public opposition to those industries—for example, through boycotts.

Abolitionist Boycotts

Although they lack the force of law, boycotts can be highly effective. Through boycotts, the public takes action that legislators won't.

Like bans, boycotts aren't necessarily abolitionist. A boycott of eggs from caged hens is "welfarist." It suggests that enslaving hens for their eggs is morally acceptable, provided that the hens aren't caged. In 2003 Compassion Over Killing (COK) asked the grocery chain Trader Joe's to stop selling eggs from caged hens. COK did *not* ask the store to stop selling *all* eggs. Implicitly, COK conveyed this message: sell only "free-range" eggs. Although COK calls its newsletter *The Abolitionist*, such an action sanctions the egg industry rather than advancing its abolition.

In contrast, a "Boycott Eggs" campaign would be anti-slavery (abolitionist), consistent with chicken emancipation. By persuading more people to stop buying eggs, it would reduce the number of suffering chickens while increasing opposition to the entire egg industry.

"Welfarists" commonly say, "Most consumers aren't ready to avoid eggs." It's advocates' job to change consumers' minds. Objecting to only those eggs that come from caged hens sends the wrong message.

Similarly to COK, Farm Sanctuary has asked restaurants not to sell "white veal," flesh from calves who were kept anemic and virtually immobilized (confined to crates so narrow that they couldn't turn around or lie with their legs outstretched). In doing this, Farm Sanctuary implies that selling *pink* "veal" (flesh from non-anemic, uncrated calves) is morally acceptable. No animal rights advocate considers flesh from *any* calf an acceptable menu item. A rights-based campaign would call for a boycott of all calf flesh, an end to the entire "veal" industry.

In addition to boycotting particular products such as eggs and calf flesh, activists can boycott particular speciesist enterprises, such as zoos, aquaprisons, circuses, rodeos, horse racing, or "swim with the dolphins" tourist attractions. Activists also can boycott particular companies, restaurants, or stores—such as body-care companies that test their products on nonhumans, restaurants heavily focused on flesh, and stores that continue to sell pelt coats. Such boycotts are directed at a form of exploitation, not the conditions under which the exploitation occurs. By all means, boycotts can and should expose those conditions, but the boycotts shouldn't be halted if the conditions of abuse are altered. A body-care company that tests on nonhumans should be boycotted whether or not the tests are performed at an especially cruel laboratory. A restaurant built on massive consumption of flesh—such as Burger King or KFC—should be boycotted whether or not it requires its flesh suppliers to confine and kill animals in accordance with so-called humane standards.

Products and institutions also can be opposed before they exist. For example, if a city or university is planning to build a new aquaprison or vivisection facility, activists can try to prevent the facility's existence.

Promoting Veganism

While seeking bans and engaging in boycotts, activists can directly promote veganism. A vegan lifestyle is an animal rights worldview put into practice. By "vegan lifestyle" I mean a commitment to avoiding products and enterprises that involve intentional, needless infliction of nonhuman suffering and death.

A vegan doesn't eat any food derived from nonhumans; wear animal-derived clothes or accessories; buy household, beauty, or body-care products that contain animal-derived ingredients or were tested on nonhumans; visit aquaprisons or zoos; contribute to organizations that fund vivisection; buy nonhumans (except to save them from abuse or death); or otherwise willingly participate in speciesist abuse. To the fullest extent possible, a vegan avoids intentional harm to nonhuman beings.

Simply publicizing the realities of nonhuman exploitation can prompt many people to become vegan. Most of the public is largely ignorant regarding the cruelty of commercial and sport fishing, "animal agriculture" and "aquaculture," hunting, vivisection, the pelt industry, the pet trade, "animal acts," dog and horse racing, and other forms of speciesist exploitation. Photos and video footage of abuse are especially powerful in motivating people to change their habits. Activists also can distribute literature that explains the moral necessity of being vegan.

In addition, activists can disseminate vegan recipes, prepare vegan food for guests, promote vegan restaurants and stores, give novices tips on vegan products, hold vegan bake sales and food festivals, and convince restaurants and stores to offer more vegan meals and products. A vegan diet offers a tremendous variety of healthful, delicious foods.

Some activists who consider themselves advocates of veganism condone eating honey or applaud people for limiting their egg consumption to "free-range eggs" and their cow-flesh consumption to "grass-fed beef." Eating honey, eggs, or cow flesh isn't vegan, so endorsing their consumption isn't veganism advocacy. Veganism advocates urge people not to eat *any* honey, eggs, or flesh. Nonvegans need to phase out or immediately eliminate animal-derived foods, not substitute some for others. It's easy to avoid eating honey, eggs, and flesh, including as ingredients. Suggesting otherwise impedes, rather than advances, veganism.

In 2003, after learning more about the food industry's treatment of nonhumans, John Mackey, CEO of Whole Foods Market, reported that he had become vegan for moral reasons. Mackey described veganism as the most compassionate lifestyle and stated, "Eating animals causes pain and suffering to the animals."[1] When I learned of Mackey's new veganism, I e-mailed all members of a Washington, D.C. "animal rights" list, urging that nonhuman-advocacy groups publicly ask Whole Foods to become a vegan store. Some individuals wrote to Mackey. Also, Friends of Animals (FoA) president Priscilla Feral sent Mackey an open letter asking that he apply his personal principles to his business and make Whole Foods "the first major vegan market in the Americas."[2] To my knowledge, no group other than FoA asked Whole Foods to end, or start phasing out, its sale of animal-derived foods. Perhaps some groups thought the request too unlikely to succeed (that belief, of course, can be self-fulfilling). Perhaps others didn't want to appear to gainsay recent "welfarist" steps taken by Whole Foods. In response to information provided by Vegetarians International Voice for Animals, Whole Foods had agreed to require that its flesh suppliers follow "humane" treatment standards, starting with ducks. Such standards don't advance veganism or nonhuman emancipation. They legitimize enslavement and slaughter. Only veganism respects nonhuman rights and rejects nonhuman enslavement.

In 2003, U.S. slaughterers killed approximately 32 birds and mammals per U.S. resident.[3] In addition, U.S. residents ate the remains of countless fishes, mollusks, and crustaceans. Persuading people to adopt a vegan diet reduces the number of nonhumans who suffer and die. It also decreases public support for food-industry enslavement and slaughter, hastening the day when they can be banned.

When people adopt a *completely* vegan lifestyle, more nonhumans are spared, because ideological veganism decreases the demand for nonhuman skin and hair, products tested on nonhumans, "entertainment" such as zoos and "animal" circuses, and all other products of speciesism.

Advocating Rights

When, and only when, someone becomes a supporter of nonhuman rights, they reject *all* forms of speciesist abuse. To build public opposition to nonhuman enslavement, activists must wage anti-slavery campaigns.

A campaign by Responsible Policies for Animals (RPA) exemplifies animal rights advocacy. In 2003, RPA executive director David Cantor wrote to the head of each U.S. state's primary land-grant university, asking them to start dismantling their school's "animal agriculture" program. Among other things, Cantor objected to the killing of nonhumans (that is, depriving them of their right to life). He told a *PRWeek* reporter, "We're an abolitionist organization. We want an end to the animal [*sic*] industry, and we want an end to the teaching of that industry."[4] No "welfarist" bargaining away of nonhuman rights. No reluctance to state the true goal ("an end to the animal industry"). An unequivocally anti-slavery stance. Cantor's efforts generated discussion that got people to question nonhuman exploitation itself.

Animal rights advocates do *not* advocate measures that violate nonhuman rights (see chapter 4). Keeping hens in cages violates their rights, but so does keeping them in cageless warehouses or breeding them in the first place. Whether or not chickens are rendered unconscious before they're slaughtered, slaughtering them violates their right to life. No *rights* advocate calls for less-cruel enslavement or slaughter. Rights advocates call for an *end* to enslavement and slaughter. They seek widespread recognition of nonhumans' moral right to life and liberty.

Years ago, animal rights activists commonly chanted, "What do we want? Animal rights! When do we want it? Now!" Today much activism could be expressed only with chants like this: "What do we want? Slightly bigger cages! When do we want them? Whenever McDonald's or some other massive abuser consents to require that their suppliers use them!" Compare the abolitionist chant "Stop Killing Chickens!" to its "welfarist" counterpart (for good reason, only imaginary): "Gas the Chickens!" Compromising on moral essentials can't inspire; it can only leave people unmoved or, worse, repel the very individuals whose moral integrity makes them prospective supporters of nonhuman rights.

By definition, animal rights advocates advocate *rights*. Individuals and groups truly committed to nonhuman emancipation don't conceal or downplay their liberationist goals when addressing people who don't support, or who actively oppose, nonhuman rights. To the contrary, they argue most forcefully against speciesism when in its presence. Instead of pandering to prevailing speciesist views, rights advocates counter them, whatever the forum. They don't equivocate but openly, firmly demand abolition. Nonhumans need clarion calls for rights, not weak requests for "welfare."

The language of abolition and rights is a crucial part of nonhuman advocacy. Animal rights groups should declare their emancipationist agenda in their names, mission statements, and literature. Names such as "Justice for All Species" and "New Jersey Animal Rights Alliance" send the right message. So do slogans such as "Rats Have Rights," "Ban Vivisection," and "Animals Are Not Ours to Eat, Wear, or Experiment On."

Animal rights advocates should apply the same vocabulary—the same strong, moralistic language—to atrocities against nonhumans as to atrocities against humans. If an act is "horrific" or "unconscionable" when committed against humans, it's equally horrific and unconscionable when committed against other animals. "Farmed" animals are imprisoned and murdered. Nonhuman advocates should say so. Hunting, fishing, and lethal trapping are murder; the perpetrators are serial killers. Slaughter and "pest control" are mass murder. Most trapping, fishing, vivisection, and food-industry confinement entail torture. Nonhumans in zoos and aquaprisons are captives, falsely imprisoned. Beating elephants, chimpanzees, and other nonhumans to "control" them and get them to perform is battery. To "tame" is to subjugate and oppress. The forced insemination of cows, dogs, and other nonhumans is sexual assault. So-called pork producers, fish farmers, and cattle ranchers are enslavers. "Animal dealers" are slave traffickers. Nonhumans are owned; our language should acknowledge that reality. (Tabooing the word *owner* denies enslavement.)

Rights advocates should bring legal cases that challenge nonhuman enslavement. In chapter 6, I described the 1980 case of *State v. LeVasseur*. Kenneth LeVasseur argued that liberating two dolphins from a vivisection lab was justified because the dolphins were persons.[5] He lost, but the case broke new ground. Decades have passed without any other U.S. case seeking to accomplish or justify nonhuman emancipation on the grounds that nonhumans are persons.

Advocates need to bring cases that assert the personhood of members of particular species. LeVasseur illegally liberated two dolphins and then sought judicial approval of his action. Advocates can continue to use that strategy. They also can seek to liberate one or more nonhumans *through* the courts, by trying to convince a judge to classify all members of a particular species as persons.

As previously discussed, cases seeking personhood for members of particular species should be based on those animals' obvious sentience. In the eyes of the law, mentally incompetent humans such as Joseph Saikewicz and Nicholas Romeo have interests that merit protection.[6] The law doesn't sanction the vivisection of humans with IQs of 10. Interests aren't contingent on intelligence, but sentience. If Saikewicz and Romeo are legal persons, and we truly value fairness, then bumblebees, stingrays, and horned toads must be legal persons too.

The sentience of a dolphin, chimpanzee, or dog should be obvious to any judge or jury with even minimal knowledge of evolution, physiology, and nonhuman behavior. If necessary, advocates can demonstrate sentience by providing compelling evidence that the animals in question think and feel. This evidence shouldn't be couched in terms of humanness—that is, genetic, intellectual, or emotional similarities to humans—but should be used to demonstrate a capacity to experience. In the case of dolphins and chimpanzees, personhood would mean a phasing out of captivity. In the case of dogs, it would mean a rapid decline in the number of dogs, whom humans no longer could legally breed, sell, or otherwise subjugate and exploit for any purpose, including as "police dogs" or "seeing-eye dogs."

Explicit advocacy of nonhuman rights and emancipation must become widespread. Otherwise, every battle against speciesist abuse will be fought separately. As of now, one animal rights group works to outlaw bear hunting; another works to end horse slaughter; another works to prevent a university from building an additional vivisection facility. Such abolitionist campaigns are entirely worthy; they don't advocate any violation of nonhuman rights. However, until more groups persistently advocate the rights of *all* nonhumans, each abuse will be hard to combat, and the list of abuses will remain hopelessly long. The only way to hasten emancipation is to convince an ever-larger segment of society that *every* form of speciesist exploitation is wrong.

Campaigning against Speciesism

Large-scale emancipation will require a change in people's attitudes. We must greatly reduce speciesism.

To do that, advocates need to campaign in nonspeciesist ways. For one thing, they need to avoid speciesist language.[7] Exploitive category terms like *poultry*, *livestock*, and *companion animals* label nonhumans for human use. Phrases such as *wildlife conservation* and *surplus dogs and cats* reduce nonhumans to commodities. Referring to nonhumans as "it," "that," and "something" equates them with insentient things. Advocates should speak of nonhumans with full respect. Instead of "dairy cows" and "broiler chickens," they should speak of "cows enslaved for their milk" and "chickens reared for slaughter." "Animals" should include humans as well as nonhumans.

Advocates also must eschew strategies inconsistent with nonhuman rights and equality. "Welfarism" is old-speciesist: it replaces particular ways of violating nonhuman rights with other ways. Anthropocentric arguments, too, perpetuate speciesism. Opposing vivisection or the flesh industry on the grounds that vivisection and flesh-eating do more harm than good to humans suggests that those practices would be acceptable if they benefited humans. Arguing that orangutans or gorillas should be legal persons because they closely resemble humans buttresses a hierarchy of worth with humans at the top and keeps rights linked to humanness.

Eliminating speciesism from our words and actions requires vigilance. Animal rights advocates should continually ask themselves, "Is my argument nonspeciesist? My language? My campaign?" If not, they should make changes. Our messages and tactics need to be consistent with our goal of eliminating speciesism. How else can we overcome this most deeply entrenched and harmful form of injustice?

In addition to campaigning in a nonspeciesist way, animal rights advocates need to campaign against speciesism itself. They should make a concerted effort to educate people about speciesism, defining the term and using it often. My first encounter with the word *speciesism* had a powerful effect on me. The concept of speciesism helped me to connect all the ways in which I had disregarded nonhumans. I hope that the word *speciesism* soon will be as familiar to the general public as *racism* and *sexism* are today.

Animal rights advocates need to write and lecture against speciesism and point it out to family, friends, co-workers, fellow advocates, and others with whom they interact. They need to explain the injustice of denying nonhumans legal rights, counter the notion of human superiority, and spread the conviction that all sentient beings are equal.

Once people recognize speciesism's inherent cruelty and injustice, there's no further need to argue issue by issue. Like rights-based arguments, the arguments against speciesism show why *all* human exploitation of nonhumans is wrong. Currently, nonhuman advocacy has too many specialists: people who focus exclusively on hunting, vivisection, dogs and cats, or birds enslaved for food. Depending on how they're carried out, such circumscribed efforts may respect nonhumans' moral rights and advance nonhuman emancipation. Ultimately, however, they can't get us where we need to go.

Until we reduce society's speciesism, we'll keep treating the symptoms rather than curing the illness. In the end, only a substantial decrease in speciesism can emancipate nonhumans.

Why emancipate nonhumans? Enslavement is wrong, murder is wrong, and causing innocent beings to suffer is wrong. Fully as much as humans, all nonhumans are entitled to life, freedom, and other basic rights. Humans deny this for only one reason: speciesism.

Notes

Preface on Language

1. See *The Merriam-Webster Concise Handbook for Writers* (Springfield, Mass.: Merriam-Webster, 1991), 83.

2. See Joan Dunayer, *Animal Equality: Language and Liberation* (Derwood, Md.: Ryce, 2001).

1 Speciesism Defined

1. See Richard Ryder, "An Autobiography," *Between the Species*, Summer 1992, 168–73, quotation at 171.

2. Peter Singer, *Animal Liberation* (New York: New York Review of Books, 1975), 7.

3. Peter Singer, "Animal Liberation at 30," *New York Review of Books*, 15 May 2003, 23–26, at 23.

4. Tom Regan, "The Case for Animal Rights," in Carl Cohen and Tom Regan, *The Animal Rights Debate* (Lanham, Md.: Rowman & Littlefield, 2001), 125–222, at 170.

5. Regan, 181.

6. Paola Cavalieri, *The Animal Question: Why Nonhuman Animals Deserve Human Rights*, 2d ed., trans. Catherine Woollard (New York: Oxford University Press, 2001), 70.

7. Cavalieri, 70.

8. Singer, "Animal Liberation at 30," 23.

9. David Nibert, *Animal Rights/Human Rights: Entanglements of Oppression and Liberation* (Lanham, Md.: Rowman & Littlefield, 2002), 243.

2 Old-Speciesist Philosophy

1. Quoted in Cleveland Amory, *Man Kind? Our Incredible War on Wildlife* (New York: Dell, 1974), 185.

2. Joe Vansickle, "Heating Tubes Top Contest," *National Hog Farmer*, 15 July 1996, 8–10, 12, at 9.

3. Malcolm Martin quoted in Michael Specter, "Lab Mishap Destroys AIDS Mice," *Washington Post*, 8 Dec. 1988, A3.

4. Chuck Mier quoted in Ron Johnson, "PETA Signs Prompt Reader to Boycott Companies," *Agri-View* (Madison, Wisc.), 13 Nov. 2003, C2.

5. James B. Whisker, *The Right to Hunt* (Croton-on-Hudson, N.Y.: North River, 1981), 97.

6. John K. Beene, "In Defense of Hunting" (letter), *Field & Stream*, Dec. 1990, 10.

7. Quoted in Mary T. Phillips, "Proper Names and the Social Construction of Biography: The Negative Case of Laboratory Animals," *Qualitative Sociology* 17, no. 2 (1994): 119–42, at 131.

8. See Phillips, "Proper Names."

9. In *Products of Pain*, videotape filmed by People for the Ethical Treatment of Animals undercover investigator Leslie Fain, compiled by Lori Gruen and Ken Knowles (Washington, D.C.: Ark II, 1986).

10. William Conway quoted in Douglas Martin, "Much More than a Zoo," *New York Times*, 25 Apr. 1995, B1, B3, at B3.

11. See Michael Lesy, *The Forbidden Zone* (New York: Farrar, Straus & Giroux, 1987), 130.

12. Joseph D. McInerney, "Animals in Education: Are We Prisoners of False Sentiment?" *American Biology Teacher*, May 1993, 276–80, at 276.

13. See, for example, Mary T. Phillips, "Savages, Drunks, and Lab Animals: The Researcher's Perception of Pain," *Society and Animals* 1, no. 1 (1993): 61–81.

14. See Linne' Hansen, "Shooting Lessons for Young Hunters," *Fur–Fish–Game*, Mar. 1993, 26–29.

15. Verl M. Thomas, *Beef Cattle Production: An Integrated Approach* (Philadelphia: Lea & Febiger, 1986), 46.

16. See Lynne U. Sneddon, Research Fellow, Animal Biology, University of Liverpool, e-mail to author, 26 Aug. 2003.

17. See American Society of Ichthyologists and Herpetologists (ASIH), American Fisheries Society, and American Institute of Fisheries Research Biologists, "Guidelines for Use of Fishes in Field Research," *Fisheries* 13, no. 2 (1988): 16–23; ASIH, Herpetologists' League, and Society for the Study of Amphibians and Reptiles, "Guidelines for Use of Live Amphibians and Reptiles in Field Research," ASIH website (http://www.asih.org/pubs/herpcoll.html), 28 Dec. 2002; American Veterinary Medical Association, "2000 Report of the AVMA Panel on Euthanasia," *Journal of the American Veterinary Medical Association*, 1 Mar. 2001, 669–96; Karen L. Machin, "Fish, Amphibian, and Reptile Analgesia," *Veterinary Clinics of North America: Exotic Animal Practice* 4, no. 1 (2001): 19–33; Margaret Rose and David Adams, "Evidence for Pain and Suffering in Other Animals," in *Animal Experimentation: The Consensus Changes*, ed. Gill Langley (New York: Macmillan, 1989), 42–71.

18. See Lynne U. Sneddon, Victoria A. Braithwaite, and Michael J. Gentle, "Do Fishes Have Nociceptors? Evidence for the Evolution of a Vertebrate Sensory System," *Proceedings of the Royal Society of London: Series B* 270, no. 1520 (2003): 1115–22.

19. See Lynne U. Sneddon, "The Evidence for Pain in Fish: The Use of Morphine as an Analgesic," *Applied Animal Behaviour Science* 83, no. 2 (2003): 153–62.

20. See Martin Kavaliers, "Evolutionary and Comparative Aspects of Nociception," *Brain Research Bulletin* 21, no. 6 (1988): 923–31; Machin.

21. See Mary Lou Hoelscher, letter, *Dairy Goat Journal*, Aug. 1986, 27, 51.

22. Steve C. Kestin, *Pain and Stress in Fish* (Horsham, England: Royal Society for the Prevention of Cruelty to Animals, 1994), 27.

23. See Kavaliers.

24. See Theodore X. Barber, *The Human Nature of Birds: A Scientific Discovery with Startling Implications* (New York: St. Martin's, 1993), 82, 84.

25. See G. M. Cronin, "The Development and Significance of Abnormal Stereotyped Behaviours in Tethered Sows" (Ph.D. diss., Agricultural University of Wageningen, Netherlands, 1985), 25, 29, 40.

26. Terrence W. Deacon, "Rethinking Mammalian Brain Evolution," *American Zoologist* 30, no. 3 (1990): 629–705, at 657.

27. Deacon, 656.

28. Ann B. Butler and William Hodos, *Comparative Vertebrate Neuroanatomy: Evolution and Adaptation* (New York: Wiley-Liss, 1996), 293.

29. Butler and Hodos, 73.

30. Sven O. E. Ebbesson, "On the Organization of the Telencephalon in Elasmobranchs," in *Comparative Neurology of the Telencephalon*, ed. Sven O. E. Ebbesson (New York: Plenum, 1980), 1–16, at 1.

31. See Hope Ryden, *Lily Pond: Four Years with a Family of Beavers* (New York: William Morrow, 1989), 25, 170–96.

32. See, for example, Francine Patterson and Eugene Linden, *The Education of Koko* (New York: Holt, Rinehart & Winston, 1981), 199–200; Ronald J. Schusterman and Kathy Krieger, "Artificial Language Comprehension and Size Transposition by a California Sea Lion (*Zalophus californianus*)," *Journal of Comparative Psychology* 100, no. 4 (1986): 348–55; Ronald A. Langworthy and Joseph W. Jennings, "Odd Ball, Abstract, Olfactory Learning in Laboratory Rats," *Psychological Record* 22, no. 4 (1972): 487–90; Hank Davis and Rachelle Pérusse, "Numerical Competence in Animals: Definitional Issues, Current Evidence, and a New Research Agenda," *Behavioral and Brain Sciences* 11, no. 4 (1988): 561–79, 611–15; David Premack and Ann J. Premack, *The Mind of an Ape* (New York: W. W. Norton, 1983), 24–26, 40–47; Irene M. Pepperberg, "Comprehension of 'Absence' by an African Grey Parrot: Learning with Respect to Questions of Same/Different," *Journal of the Experimental Analysis of Behavior* 50, no. 3 (1988): 553–64.

33. See C. N. Slobodchikoff, C. Fischer, and J. Shapiro, "Predator-Specific Words in Prairie Dog Alarm Calls," Abstract 557, *American Zoologist* 26 (1986): 105A; C. N. Slobodchikoff et al., "Semantic Information Distinguishing Individual Predators in the Alarm Calls of Gunnison's Prairie Dogs," *Animal Behaviour* 42, no. 5 (1991): 713–19.

34. See Francine Patterson and Wendy Gordon, "The Case for the Personhood of Gorillas," in *The Great Ape Project: Equality beyond Humanity*, ed. Paola Cavalieri and Peter Singer (New York: St. Martin's, 1993), 58–77.

35. See *Youngberg v. Romeo*, 457 U.S. Reports 307–31 (1982).

36. See Patterson and Gordon.

37. *American Heritage Dictionary*, 3d ed., under *brute*.

38. See Philip Gonzalez and Leonore Fleischer, *The Dog Who Rescues Cats: The True Story of Ginny* (New York: HarperCollins, 1995), 27–34, 47–53, 57–58, quotation at 67.

39. See Stanley Milgram, "Behavioral Study of Obedience," *Journal of Abnormal and Social Psychology* 67, no. 4 (1963): 371–78.

40. See Jules H. Masserman, Stanley Wechkin, and William Terris, "'Altruistic' Behavior in Rhesus Monkeys," *American Journal of Psychiatry* 121 (1964): 584–85.

41. See Steve F. Sapontzis, *Morals, Reason, and Animals* (Philadelphia: Temple University Press, 1987), 27, 45.

3 Old-Speciesist Law

1. See Victoria Benning, "Front Royal Magistrate Faces Cat-Nabbing Charges," *Washington Post*, 7 Aug. 1996, D2.

2. See Gary L. Francione, *Animals, Property, and the Law* (Philadelphia: Temple University Press, 1995), 91.

3. See "New Claims Reveal the Endless Potential for Human Injury," *Professional Liability: The AVMA Trust Report* (American Veterinary Medical Association), Sept. 1991, 1.

4. *Tennessee Code*, sec. 39-14-205.

5. Seymour Friedman quoted in *Corso v. Crawford Dog and Cat Hospital, Inc.*, 415 New York Supplement, 2d ser., 182–83 (New York City Civil Court 1979), at 183.

6. Eric Andell quoted in *Bueckner v. Hamel*, 886 South Western Reporter, 2d ser., 368–78 (Tex. Court of Appeals—Houston [1st District] 1994), at 377, 378, 377.

7. William Bablitch quoted in *Rabideau v. City of Racine*, 627 North Western Reporter, 2d ser., 795–807 (Wisc. Supreme Court 2001), at 798.

8. Shirley Abrahamson quoted in *Rabideau v. City of Racine*, 806.

9. *U.S. Code*, title 16, sec. 1361.

10. *U.S. Code*, title 16, sec. 1411.

11. *U.S. Code*, title 16, sec. 1372.

12. See *U.S. Code*, title 16, sec. 1412.

13. See *U.S. Code*, title 16, sec. 1389.

14. *U.S. Code*, title 16, sec. 1378.

15. *U.S. Code*, title 16, sec. 1374.

16. See Harold W. Thompson, *Body, Boots and Britches: Folktales, Ballads and Speech from Country New York* (1939; reprint, Syracuse, N.Y.: Syracuse University Press, 1979), 67.

17. *U.S. Code*, title 16, sec. 1531.

18. Bernard E. Rollin, *Animal Rights and Human Morality*, 2d ed. (Buffalo, N.Y.: Prometheus, 1992), 104.

19. See *Pennsylvania Consolidated Statutes*, title 18, sec. 5511.

20. *Texas Codes: Penal Code*, title 9, sec. 42.09; *Utah Code*, sec. 76-9-301; *Tennessee Code*, sec. 39-14-202.

21. See Francione, *Animals, Property, and the Law*, 129–30, 139–56. Also see David J. Wolfson, *Beyond the Law: Agribusiness and the Systemic Abuse of Animals Raised for Food or Food Production*, 2d ed. (Watkins Glen, N.Y.: Farm Sanctuary, 1999).

22. See *Iowa Code*, title 16, secs. 481A.1, 717.1, 717B.1.

23. See Lynn S. Branham, *The Law of Sentencing, Corrections, and Prisoners' Rights: In a Nutshell*, 6th ed. (St. Paul, Minn.: West Group, 2002), 274–98.

24. Estimate provided by Norm Phelps of the Fund for Animals, 29 Mar. 2000, and based primarily on 1996–97 data from state "wildlife" agencies and 1998–99 data from the U.S. Fish and Wildlife Service. See Fund for Animals, *Body Count: The Death Toll in America's War on Wildlife* (New York: Fund for Animals, 2000).

25. David E. Petzal, "Two Modest Proposals," *Field & Stream*, July 1990, 26, 35, at 26.

26. *Maine Revised Statutes*, title 17, sec. 1037.

27. See Branham, 288–89.

28. *South Dakota Codified Laws*, sec. 40-1-2.4.

29. See Francione, *Animals, Property, and the Law*, 129–30, 139–56.

30. See Ivette Mendez, "Pair Fined for 'House with Dead Animals,'" *Star-Ledger* (Newark, N.J.), 24 July 1996, 51.

31. See Donald F. Patterson, "Epidemiologic and Genetic Studies of Congenital Heart Disease in the Dog," *Circulation Research* 23 (1968): 171–202.

32. See George A. Padgett, "Genetics: Specifically Regarding Cataracts," *Kennel Doctor*, June 1988, 4–6.

33. Francione, *Animals, Property, and the Law*, 129; Gary L. Francione, *Introduction to Animal Rights: Your Child or the Dog?* (Philadelphia: Temple University Press, 2000), 55.

34. See Francione, *Animals, Property, and the Law*, 129–30, 139–56.

35. *Code of Federal Regulations*, title 9, secs. 3.28, 3.53, 3.80, 3.128.

36. See Ros Clubb and Georgia Mason, "Captivity Effects on Wide-Ranging Carnivores," *Nature*, 2 Oct. 2003, 473–74.

37. See American Society for the Prevention of Cruelty to Animals (ASPCA), Fund for Animals (FFA), and Animal Welfare Institute (AWI), *Government Sanctioned Abuse: How the United States Department of Agriculture Allows Ringling Brothers Circus to Systematically Mistreat Elephants* (New York: ASPCA, FFA, and AWI, 2003).

38. See Jane Fritsch, "Elephants in Captivity: A Dark Side," *Los Angeles Times*, 5 Oct. 1988, sec. 1, pp. 1+; Jane Fritsch, "Keepers Struck Elephant More than 100 Times, Trainer Says," *Los Angeles Times*, 26 May 1988, sec. 1, pp. 3, 33; Jane Fritsch, "Zoo Official Says Wild Animal Park Trainers Injured Aggressive Elephant," *Los Angeles Times*, 25 May 1988, sec. 1, pp. 3, 20; Bernard Gavzer, "Are Our Zoos Humane?" *Parade Magazine*, 26 Mar. 1989, 4–9; "Loading Lota," *Milwaukee Sentinel*, 28 Nov. 1990, sec. 1, p. 1; Michael Winikoff, "Lota Lost?" *HSUS News* (Humane Society of the United States), Spring 1992, 22–26; ASPCA, FFA, and AWI.

39. *U.S. Code*, title 7, sec. 2132.

40. See *Animal Legal Defense Fund v. Madigan*, 781 Federal Supplement 797–806 (District Court, D.C. 1992).

41. See Shanaz M. Tejani-Butt, William P. Paré, and J. Yang, "Effect of Repeated Novel Stressors on Depressive Behavior and Brain Norepinephrine Receptor System in Sprague-Dawley and Wistar Kyoto (WKY) Rats," *Brain Research* 649, nos. 1–2 (1994): 27–35.

42. See National Marine Fisheries Service, *Fisheries of the United States, 2002* (Silver Spring, Md.: U.S. Department of Commerce, 2003), 3–4.

43. See Peter Singer and Karen Dawn, "Back at the Ranch: A Horror Story," *Los Angeles Times* (home ed.), 1 Dec. 2003, Metro sec., part 2, p. 11.

44. See National Agricultural Statistics Service (NASS), *Catfish Production*, Feb. 2004, 11, 15; NASS, *Livestock Slaughter: 2003 Summary*, Mar. 2004, 1; NASS, *Poultry Slaughter: 2003 Annual Summary*, Mar. 2004, 2–3; NASS, *Trout Production*, Feb. 2004, 6, 10.

45. See NASS, *Poultry Slaughter*, 2.

46. See NASS, *Poultry Slaughter*, 3.

47. See Gail A. Eisnitz, *Slaughterhouse: The Shocking Story of Greed, Neglect, and Inhumane Treatment inside the U.S. Meat Industry* (Amherst, N.Y.: Prometheus, 1997), 166, 194, 280.

48. See United Poultry Concerns (UPC), "United Poultry Concerns Calls on Tyson Foods, KFC, and the National Chicken Council to Improve Bird Welfare and Set Policies Prohibiting Deliberate Cruelty to Chickens" (news release), UPC, Machipongo, Va., 1 Apr. 2003.

49. See NASS, *Catfish Production*, 11, 15.

50. See NASS, *Trout Production*, 6, 10.

51. See NASS, *Livestock Slaughter*, 1.

52. *U.S. Code*, title 7, sec. 1902.

53. See Eisnitz, 20, 25, 28–29, 41–44, 120–24, 126–30, 132–33, 144–45, 197–98, 200, 203–4, 215–17, 223; Joby Warrick, "'They Die Piece by Piece,'" *Washington Post*, 10 Apr. 2001, A1, A10.

54. See Eisnitz, 66–75, 80, 83–88, 90–94, 97–98, 133, 143–44, 237, 265–66; Temple Grandin, "Euthanasia and Slaughter of Livestock," *Journal of the American Veterinary Medical Association*, 1 May 1994, 1354–60.

55. See Eisnitz, 93–94, 98, 144–45; Temple Grandin, "Behavior of Slaughter Plant and Auction Employees toward the Animals," *Anthrozoös* 1, no. 4 (1988): 205–13.

56. See David Foster, "Animal Rights Activists Getting Message Across," *Chicago Tribune* (evening ed.), 25 Jan. 1996, 8.

4 Old-Speciesist Advocacy

1. See "Molecules and Markets: A Survey of Pharmaceuticals," *Economist*, 7 Feb. 1987, 14-page insert between pp. 50 and 51; John Schwartz, "Fat-Fighting Drug Shows Results in First Human Trial," *Washington Post*, 15 June 1998, A14.

2. George Bernard Shaw, "Preface on Doctors," in *The Doctor's Dilemma: A Tragedy* (1911; reprint, Baltimore: Penguin, 1954), 7–88, at 53.

3. See Gary L. Francione, *Rain without Thunder: The Ideology of the Animal Rights Movement* (Philadelphia: Temple University Press, 1996), 118.

4. Jonathan Balcombe, "Verbal Vivisection: Comments on Dunayer's 'In the Name of Science,'" *Organization and Environment* 13, no. 4 (2000): 460–62, at 462.

5. Andrew N. Rowan, *Of Mice, Models, and Men: A Critical Evaluation of Animal Research* (Albany: State University of New York Press, 1984), 3 (also see 23).

6. *American Heritage Dictionary*, 3d ed., under *pet*.

7. See Gary L. Francione, *Introduction to Animal Rights: Your Child or the Dog?* (Philadelphia: Temple University Press, 2000), xxxv.

8. Francione, *Introduction to Animal Rights*, 204 n. 59.

9. For example, Francione, *Introduction to Animal Rights*, 21, 22, 25.

10. For example, Francione, *Introduction to Animal Rights*, 25, 28, 19.

11. Francione, *Introduction to Animal Rights*, 115.

12. Wiley A. Hall III, "A Boiling Issue to Chew Over," *PETA News* (People for the Ethical Treatment of Animals), July/Aug. 1989, 5.

13. Jim Motavalli, "They Eat Horses, Don't They?" *Animals' Agenda*, Nov./Dec. 1992, 16–22; Virginia Bollinger, "You Can Lead a Horse to Slaughter," *Animals' Agenda*, May/June 1994, 10–12.

14. Francione, *Rain without Thunder*, 2.

15. Steven Slosberg, "For Animals' Sake She Pulled the Trigger," *The Day* (New London, Conn.), 30 Nov. 2003, D1.

16. Slosberg.

17. See "Americans Oppose Egg Factory Farming," *Farm Sanctuary News*, Spring 2001, 7.

18. Stephanie Simon, "Killing Them Softly," *Los Angeles Times*, 29 Apr. 2003, A1, A18, at A18.

19. Elizabeth Weise, "Food Sellers Push Animal Welfare," *USA Today*, 13 Aug. 2003, D1–D2, at D1.

20. Chuck Mier quoted in Ron Johnson, "PETA Signs Prompt Reader to Boycott Companies," *Agri-View* (Madison, Wisc.), 13 Nov. 2003, C2.

21. Jay Nordlinger, "PETA vs. KFC," *National Review*, 22 Dec. 2003, 27.

22. David Nibert, *Animal Rights/Human Rights: Entanglements of Oppression and Liberation* (Lanham, Md.: Rowman & Littlefield, 2002), 252.

23. Sean Day, e-mail to author, 8 July 2003.

24. Francione, *Rain without Thunder*, 44, 239 n. 36.

25. Karen Davis quoted in United Poultry Concerns (UPC), "United Poultry Concerns Calls on Tyson Foods, KFC, and the National Chicken Council to Improve Bird Welfare and Set Policies Prohibiting Deliberate Cruelty to Chickens" (news release), UPC, Machipongo, Va., 1 Apr. 2003.

26. See Francione, *Rain without Thunder*, 6.

27. Nibert, 164.

28. Joyce Tischler quoted in R. Scott Nolen, "Lawsuit Seeks Stronger Protections for Primates," *Journal of the American Veterinary Medical Association*, 1 Dec. 2003, 1543–44, at 1544.

29. Francione, *Rain without Thunder*, 116.

30. Nibert, 167.

31. See Rod Smith, "Egg Producers Receive Recommendations for Four Non-Feed-Withdrawal Molt Diets," *Feedstuffs*, 5 Apr. 2004, 8, 11.

32. See Smith.

33. See Paul Shapiro, e-mail to author, 25 June 2003.

34. Smith, 8.

35. Francione, *Introduction to Animal Rights*, 55.

36. See National Agricultural Statistics Service, *Chickens and Eggs*, May 2004, 2.

37. See, for example, Francione, *Rain without Thunder*, 208.

38. See Francione, *Rain without Thunder*, 190.

39. Francione, *Rain without Thunder*, 215.

40. Francione, *Rain without Thunder*, 202 (also see 210).

41. Francione, *Rain without Thunder*, 202–3.

42. Francione, *Rain without Thunder*, 207, 210.

43. Francione, *Rain without Thunder*, 215, 216.

44. See Francione, *Rain without Thunder*, 210.

45. See Francione, *Rain without Thunder*, 214.

46. Karen Davis quoted in UPC, "United Poultry Concerns Calls on Tyson Foods."

47. UPC, "United Poultry Concerns Reports a Successful Student Protest against the New Hampshire SPCA's Use of Suffering Animals to Raise Shelter Funds" (news release), UPC, Machipongo, Va., 17 Nov. 2003.

48. Bruce Friedrich, e-mail to AR-News, 23 Nov. 2003.

49. See Francione, *Rain without Thunder*, 113.

5 New-Speciesist Philosophy

1. Peter Singer, *Animal Liberation*, 2d ed. (New York: New York Review of Books, 1990), 3.

2. Peter Singer, *Practical Ethics*, 2d ed. (Cambridge: Cambridge University Press, 1993), 58, 131.

3. Singer, *Animal Liberation*, 239.

4. Peter Singer quoted in Scott Allen, "Apes on Edge," *Boston Globe*, 7 Nov. 1994, 1, 12, at 12.

5. Singer, *Practical Ethics*, 132.

6. Singer, *Practical Ethics*, 132.

7. Singer, *Practical Ethics*, 131.

8. See Singer, *Animal Liberation*, 229–30, quotation at 230.

9. Singer, *Practical Ethics*, 133.

10. Singer, *Animal Liberation*, 229.

11. Singer, *Practical Ethics*, 120; Singer, *Animal Liberation*, 228 (also see 20).

12. Singer, *Animal Liberation*, 19.

13. Singer, *Practical Ethics*, 119.

14. Singer, *Practical Ethics*, 126.

15. Singer, *Practical Ethics*, 126.

16. See Jennifer L. Kelley and Anne E. Magurran, "Learned Predator Recognition and Antipredator Responses in Fishes," *Fish and Fisheries* 4, no. 3 (2003): 216–26.

17. See Mark Sosin and John Clark, *Through the Fish's Eye: An Angler's Guide to Gamefish Behavior* (New York: Harper & Row, 1973), 148–49.

18. See Felicity Huntingford, "Foreword," *Fish and Fisheries* 4, no. 3 (2003): 197–98.

19. Kevin N. Laland, Culum Brown, and Jens Krause, "Learning in Fishes: From Three-Second Memory to Culture," *Fish and Fisheries* 4, no. 3 (2003): 199–202, at 202.

20. Huntingford, 197.

21. Laland, Brown, and Krause, 200, 199.

22. Cristina Broglio, Fernando Rodríguez, and Cosme Salas, "Spatial Cognition and Its Neural Basis in Teleost Fishes," *Fish and Fisheries* 4, no. 3 (2003): 247–55, at 253.

23. Singer, *Animal Liberation*, 228.

24. See Singer, *Practical Ethics*, 90, 101.

25. See Singer, *Animal Liberation*, 19, 21.

26. Singer, *Practical Ethics*, 131.

27. See Singer, *Practical Ethics*, 95.

28. Singer, *Practical Ethics*, 97.

29. See Steve F. Sapontzis, *Morals, Reason, and Animals* (Philadelphia: Temple University Press, 1987), 168.

30. See Sapontzis, *Morals, Reason, and Animals*, 186.

31. Sapontzis, *Morals, Reason, and Animals*, 169.

32. Steve F. Sapontzis, "Aping Persons—Pro and Con," in *The Great Ape Project: Equality beyond Humanity*, ed. Paola Cavalieri and Peter Singer (New York: St. Martin's, 1993), 269–77, at 272.

33. Peter Singer, "Animal Liberation at 30," *New York Review of Books*, 15 May 2003, 23–26, at 25.

34. See Singer, *Practical Ethics*, 90.

35. Singer, *Practical Ethics*, 95.

36. Singer, *Practical Ethics*, 90.

37. See Mark Rowlands, *Animals Like Us* (London: Verso, 2002), 82.

38. Rowlands, 83.

39. Rowlands, 147.

40. Evelyn B. Pluhar, *Beyond Prejudice: The Moral Significance of Human and Nonhuman Animals* (Durham, N.C.: Duke University Press, 1995), 293.

41. Peter Singer, "*Animal Equality: Language and Liberation* by Joan Dunayer" (book review), *Vegan Voice*, Dec. 2001–Feb. 2002, 36.

42. See Peter Marler, "Social Cognition: Are Primates Smarter than Birds?" *Current Ornithology* 13 (1996): 1–32.

43. Maurice Burton, *Just Like an Animal* (New York: Charles Scribner's Sons, 1978), 72.

44. Singer, *Practical Ethics*, 76.

45. Sapontzis, *Morals, Reason, and Animals*, 222.

46. Singer, *Animal Liberation*, 222.

47. Singer, *Practical Ethics*, 61.

48. See Anthony A. Wright, Robert G. Cook, and Jacquelyne J. Rivera, "Concept Learning by Pigeons: Matching-to-Sample with Trial-Unique Video Picture Stimuli," *Animal Learning and Behavior* 16, no. 4 (1988): 436–44; Martin Giurfa et al., "The Concepts of 'Sameness' and 'Difference' in an Insect," *Nature*, 19 Apr. 2001, 930–33.

49. James Rachels, *Created from Animals: The Moral Implications of Darwinism* (Oxford: Oxford University Press, 1990), 57.

50. See Irene M. Pepperberg, "Numerical Competence in an African Gray Parrot (*Psittacus erithacus*)," *Journal of Comparative Psychology* 108, no. 1 (1994): 36–44.

51. See Alex Kirby, "Parrot's Oratory Stuns Scientists," *BBC News Online* (http://news.bbc.co.uk), 26 Jan. 2004.

52. Singer, *Practical Ethics*, 56, 60.

53. Rachels, 57.

54. Rowlands, 43.

55. Singer, *Animal Liberation*, 20, 21.

56. Singer, *Animal Liberation*, 21, 19.

57. Singer, *Animal Liberation*, 6.

58. Singer, *Animal Liberation*, 21.

59. See Rowlands, 46.

60. Rachels, 208.

61. Rachels, 209.

62. Rachels, 198.

63. Rachels, 64.

64. See Rachels, 70.

65. Kevin Warburton, "Learning of Foraging Skills by Fish," *Fish and Fisheries* 4, no. 3 (2003): 203–15, at 212.

66. Rachels, 208.
67. Rachels, 209.
68. Rachels, 189.
69. See Rachels, 189–90.
70. Sapontzis, *Morals, Reason, and Animals*, 219.
71. Rowlands, 98.
72. See Rachels, 180–81.
73. Singer, *Practical Ethics*, 86.
74. Singer, *Animal Liberation*, 21.
75. Paola Cavalieri, *The Animal Question: Why Nonhuman Animals Deserve Human Rights*, 2d ed., trans. Catherine Woollard (New York: Oxford University Press, 2001), 110.
76. See Tom Regan, "The Case for Animal Rights," in Carl Cohen and Tom Regan, *The Animal Rights Debate* (Lanham, Md.: Rowman & Littlefield, 2001), 125–222, at 209.
77. Tom Regan, *The Case for Animal Rights* (Berkeley: University of California Press, 1983), 262; Regan, "Case for Animal Rights," in Cohen and Regan, 211.
78. Regan, *Case for Animal Rights*, 244; see Regan, "Case for Animal Rights," in Cohen and Regan, 216.
79. Regan, *Case for Animal Rights*, 243.
80. Regan, "Case for Animal Rights," in Cohen and Regan, 209.
81. See Regan, *Case for Animal Rights*, 366.
82. See American Society of Ichthyologists and Herpetologists (ASIH), American Fisheries Society, and American Institute of Fisheries Research Biologists, "Guidelines for Use of Fishes in Field Research," *Fisheries* 13, no. 2 (1988): 16–23; ASIH, Herpetologists' League, and Society for the Study of Amphibians and Reptiles, "Guidelines for Use of Live Amphibians and Reptiles in Field Research," ASIH website (http://www.asih.org/pubs/herpcoll.html), 28 Dec. 2002; American Veterinary Medical Association, "2000 Report of the AVMA Panel on Euthanasia," *Journal of the American Veterinary Medical Association*, 1 Mar. 2001, 669–96; Karen L. Machin, "Fish, Amphibian, and Reptile Analgesia," *Veterinary Clinics of North America: Exotic Animal Practice* 4, no. 1 (2001): 19–33; Margaret Rose and David Adams, "Evidence for Pain and Suffering in Other Animals," in *Animal Experimentation: The Consensus Changes*, ed. Gill Langley (New York: Macmillan, 1989), 42–71.
83. Pluhar, 269.
84. Pluhar, 258.
85. Regan, "Case for Animal Rights," in Cohen and Regan, 215.
86. See National Agricultural Statistics Service, *Honey*, Feb. 2004, 1. According to Diana Sammataro, a research entomologist at the U.S. Department of Agriculture's Carl Hayden Bee Research Center, within the U.S. honey industry a honeybee colony averages about 60,000 bees at peak honey-production time (e-mail to author, 4 June 2004).
87. Tom Regan, "Reply to Carl Cohen," in Cohen and Regan, 263–310, at 296.
88. Regan, "Case for Animal Rights," in Cohen and Regan, 210.
89. See Regan, *Case for Animal Rights*, 366.
90. Pluhar, 259.
91. Pluhar, 259.
92. Pluhar, 259.
93. Regan, *Case for Animal Rights*, 119.

94. Regan, *Case for Animal Rights*, 324.
95. Regan, *Case for Animal Rights*, 325.
96. Gary L. Francione, *Introduction to Animal Rights: Your Child or the Dog?* (Philadelphia: Temple University Press, 2000), 151.
97. Francione, xxii.
98. Francione, 152.
99. Francione, 159.
100. Francione, 152.
101. Regan, *Case for Animal Rights*, 324.
102. See Regan, *Case for Animal Rights*, 325.
103. Regan, "Case for Animal Rights," in Cohen and Regan, 198; Regan, *Case for Animal Rights*, 297.
104. Regan, *Case for Animal Rights*, 346.
105. Rowlands, 50 (also see 34).
106. Rowlands, 54, 71.
107. Rowlands, 71.
108. Tom Regan, "The Case for Animal Rights: A Decade's Passing," in *A Quarter Century of Value Inquiry: Presidential Addresses of the American Society for Value Inquiry*, ed. Richard T. Hull (Amsterdam: Rodopi, 1994), 439–59, at 442.
109. See Sapontzis, *Morals, Reason, and Animals*, 225–26.

6 New-Speciesist Law

1. *Bailey v. Poindexter's Executor*, 55 Reports of Cases in the Supreme Court of Appeals of Virginia (14 Grattan's Virginia Reports) 428–55 (1858), at 432, 434.
2. *Commonwealth v. Welosky*, 177 North Eastern Reporter 656–65 (Mass. Supreme Court 1931), at 659, 660.
3. See Gavin Daws, "'Animal Liberation' as Crime: The Hawaii Dolphin Case," in *Ethics and Animals*, ed. Harlan B. Miller and William H. Williams (Clifton, N.J.: Humana, 1983), 361–71; *State v. LeVasseur*, 613 Pacific Reporter, 2d ser., 1328–35 (Hawaii Appellate Court 1980), quotation at 1330.
4. Steven M. Wise, *Rattling the Cage: Toward Legal Rights for Animals* (Cambridge, Mass.: Perseus, 2000), 237.
5. Steven M. Wise, *Drawing the Line: Science and the Case for Animal Rights* (Cambridge, Mass.: Perseus, 2002), 8, 6.
6. See Wise, *Drawing the Line*, 32, 231.
7. See Wise, *Drawing the Line*, 169.
8. Wise, *Drawing the Line*, 241.
9. Wise, *Drawing the Line*, 129.
10. Wise, *Drawing the Line*, 231, 241.
11. See Wise, *Drawing the Line*, 112, 178, 241.
12. See Wise, *Drawing the Line*, 178.
13. Wise, *Drawing the Line*, 7.
14. See Wise, *Rattling the Cage*, 5; Steven M. Wise, presentation at Fifteenth Annual International Compassionate Living Festival, Raleigh, N.C., 6 Oct. 2000.
15. See James L. Gould and Carol Grant Gould, *The Honey Bee* (New York: Scientific American Library, 1988), 28, 65–66.
16. See James L. Gould, "Natural History of Honey Bee Learning," in *The Biol-

ogy of Learning, ed. Peter Marler and Herbert S. Terrace (Berlin: Springer, 1984), 149–80.

17. Wise, *Drawing the Line*, 73.

18. See Wise, *Drawing the Line*, 85.

19. Wise, *Drawing the Line*, 7.

20. See Wise, *Drawing the Line*, 112.

21. Wise, *Drawing the Line*, 36.

22. Charles Darwin to J. D. Hooker, 30 Dec. 1858, *More Letters of Charles Darwin: A Record of His Work in a Series of Hitherto Unpublished Letters*, vol. 1, ed. Francis Darwin and A. C. Seward (London: John Murray, 1903), 114.

23. See *More Letters*, 114 n. 2.

24. Euan M. Macphail, *Brain and Intelligence in Vertebrates* (Oxford: Clarendon, 1982), 331; William Hodos, "Evolutionary Interpretation of Neural and Behavioral Studies of Living Vertebrates," in *The Neurosciences: Second Study Program*, ed. Francis O. Schmitt (New York: Rockefeller University Press, 1970), 26–39, at 27.

25. Wise, *Drawing the Line*, 45.

26. Wise, *Drawing the Line*, 36.

27. See Wise, *Drawing the Line*, 212.

28. Wise, *Drawing the Line*, 6, 7, 236.

29. Wise, *Drawing the Line*, 236.

30. See Wise, *Drawing the Line*, 39–41, 231.

31. See Wise, *Drawing the Line*, 34.

32. See Wise, *Drawing the Line*, 237.

33. *Superintendent of Belchertown v. Saikewicz*, 370 North Eastern Reporter, 2d ser., 417–35 (Mass. Supreme Court 1977), at 422, 423, 430.

34. *Superintendent of Belchertown v. Saikewicz*, 420.

35. *Superintendent of Belchertown v. Saikewicz*, 427, 431, 418.

36. *Superintendent of Belchertown v. Saikewicz*, 431.

37. *Youngberg v. Romeo*, 457 U.S. Reports 307–31 (1982), at 309.

38. *Youngberg v. Romeo*, 319.

39. Lee Hall and Anthony Jon Waters, "From Property to Person: The Case of Evelyn Hart," *Seton Hall Constitutional Law Journal* 11, no. 1 (2000): 1–68, at 13.

40. Wise, *Drawing the Line*, 45.

41. Alex the African gray parrot quoted in Jeffrey M. Masson and Susan McCarthy, *When Elephants Weep: The Emotional Lives of Animals* (New York: Delacorte, 1995), 35.

42. See Kenn Kaufman, "The Subject Is Alex," *Audubon*, Sept./Oct. 1991, 52–58.

43. Ariela J. Gross, "Litigating Whiteness: Trials of Racial Determination in the Nineteenth-Century South," *Yale Law Journal* 108, no. 1 (1998): 109–88, at 112, 163.

44. See *Daniel v. Guy*, 19 Arkansas Reports 121–31 (1857).

45. See back jacket of Wise, *Drawing the Line*.

7 New-Speciesist Advocacy

1. Paola Cavalieri, Peter Singer, et al., "A Declaration on Great Apes," in *The Great Ape Project: Equality beyond Humanity*, ed. Paola Cavalieri and Peter Singer (New York: St. Martin's, 1993), 4–7, at 4.

2. Paola Cavalieri and Peter Singer, "The Great Ape Project—and Beyond," in *Great Ape Project*, 304–12, at 311; Great Ape Project (GAP) website (http://www.greatapeproject.org/gapfaq.html), 10 Aug. 2003.

3. GAP website.

4. GAP website.

5. Cavalieri, Singer, et al., 5.

6. GAP website.

7. GAP website.

8. Cavalieri and Singer, "Great Ape Project," 309.

9. GAP website.

10. Cavalieri, Singer, et al., 5.

11. Paola Cavalieri and Peter Singer, "Preface," in *Great Ape Project*, 1–3, at 1.

12. Gary L. Francione, "Personhood, Property and Legal Competence," in *Great Ape Project*, 248–57, at 256.

13. Steve F. Sapontzis, "Aping Persons—Pro and Con," in *Great Ape Project*, 269–77, at 271.

14. GAP website.

15. See GAP website.

16. Cavalieri and Singer, "Great Ape Project," 309.

17. *Superintendent of Belchertown v. Saikewicz*, 370 North Eastern Reporter, 2d ser., 417–35 (Mass. Supreme Court 1977), at 427, 431, 418. Also see *Youngberg v. Romeo*, 457 U.S. Reports 307–31 (1982).

8 Nonspeciesist Philosophy

1. Steve F. Sapontzis, *Morals, Reason, and Animals* (Philadelphia: Temple University Press, 1987), 165.

2. See Gary L. Francione, *Introduction to Animal Rights: Your Child or the Dog?* (Philadelphia: Temple University Press, 2000), xxxii.

3. Francione, *Introduction to Animal Rights*, xxix.

4. Gary L. Francione, e-mail to author, 29 Feb. 2004.

5. See Steve F. Sapontzis, "Aping Persons—Pro and Con," in *The Great Ape Project: Equality beyond Humanity*, ed. Paola Cavalieri and Peter Singer (New York: St. Martin's, 1993), 269–77, quotation at 275.

6. Paola Cavalieri, *The Animal Question: Why Nonhuman Animals Deserve Human Rights*, 2d ed., trans. Catherine Woollard (New York: Oxford University Press, 2001), 139 (also see 140).

7. See Cavalieri, 142.

8. Francione, *Introduction to Animal Rights*, 6.

9. Francione, *Introduction to Animal Rights*, 176.

10. Francione, *Introduction to Animal Rights*, 6.

11. Francione, *Introduction to Animal Rights*, 190 n. 15.

12. Francione, *Introduction to Animal Rights*, xxiii, xxxvi, 190 n. 15.

13. See Laura M. Harrison et al., "The Opiate System in Invertebrates," *Peptides* 15, no. 7 (1994): 1309–29; Graziano Fiorito, "Is There 'Pain' in Invertebrates?" *Behavioural Processes* 12 (1986): 383–88.

14. See Harrison et al.

15. See Patrick Bateson, "Assessment of Pain in Animals," *Animal Behaviour* 42 (1991): 827–39; Randolf Menzel et al., "Biology of Invertebrate Learning: Group Report," in *The Biology of Learning*, ed. Peter Marler and Herbert S. Terrace (Berlin: Springer, 1984), 249–70.

16. See Martin Kavaliers, "Evolutionary and Comparative Aspects of Nociception," *Brain Research Bulletin* 21, no. 6 (1988): 923–31.

17. See C. H. Eisemann et al., "Do Insects Feel Pain?—A Biological View," *Experientia* (now *Cellular and Molecular Life Sciences*) 40 (1984): 164–67.

18. V. B. Wigglesworth, "Do Insects Feel Pain?" *Antenna* 4 (1980): 8–9, at 9.

19. Wigglesworth, 9.

20. See Fiorito; Harrison et al.

21. See Kavaliers.

22. See Menzel et al.

23. See Bernard E. Rollin, *Animal Rights and Human Morality*, 2d ed. (Buffalo, N.Y.: Prometheus, 1992), 64.

24. See Christie L. Sahley and Donald F. Ready, "Associative Learning Modifies Two Behaviors in the Leech, *Hirudo medicinalis*," *Journal of Neuroscience* 8, no. 12 (1988): 4612–20.

25. See Kavaliers.

26. Rollin, 78.

27. See Fiorito.

28. See Kavaliers.

29. See John V. Haralson, Charlene I. Groff, and Sally J. Haralson, "Classical Conditioning in the Sea Anemone, *Cribrina xanthogrammica*," *Physiology and Behavior* 15, no. 4 (1975): 455–60.

30. John E. Dowling, *Neurons and Networks: An Introduction to Neuroscience* (Cambridge, Mass.: Harvard University Press, 1992), 214.

31. Heinrich Reichert, *Introduction to Neurobiology*, trans. G. S. Boyan (Stuttgart: Georg Thieme, 1992), 4.

32. Jane A. Smith and Kenneth M. Boyd, eds., *Lives in the Balance: The Ethics of Using Animals in Biomedical Research* (Oxford: Oxford University Press, 1991), 47.

33. See Benjamin B. Beck, *Animal Tool Behavior: The Use and Manufacture of Tools by Animals* (New York: Garland, 1980), 19.

34. See Fiorito.

35. See P. B. Dews, "Some Observations on an Operant in the Octopus," *Journal of the Experimental Analysis of Behavior* 2, no. 1 (1959): 57–63, quotation at 62.

36. See Donald R. Griffin, *Animal Minds* (Chicago: University of Chicago Press, 1992), 199.

37. See Beck, 18, 19, 106.

38. Bruno van Swinderen and Ralph J. Greenspan, "Salience Modulates 20–30 Hz Brain Activity in *Drosophila*," *Nature Neuroscience* 6, no. 6 (2003): 579–86, at 579.

39. van Swinderen and Greenspan, 579. Also see Randolf Menzel and Martin Giurfa, "Cognitive Architecture of a Mini-Brain: The Honeybee," *Trends in Cognitive Sciences* 5, no. 2 (2001): 62–71.

40. See Scott Waddell and William G. Quinn, "Flies, Genes, and Learning," *Annual Review of Neuroscience* 24 (2001): 1283–1309, quotation at 1284.

41. See R. S. Newall, "Carnivorous Wasps," *Nature*, 25 Mar. 1880, 494.

42. See Erasmus Darwin, *Zoonomia; or, The Laws of Organic Life*, vol. 1 (1794–96; reprint, New York: AMS, 1974), 183.

43. See "Habits and Intelligence of *Vespa maculata*," *Proceedings of the Academy of Natural Sciences of Philadelphia*, 22 Jan. 1878, 15.

44. See Beck, 17, 194.

45. See R. Stimson Wilcox and Robert R. Jackson, "Cognitive Abilities of Araneophagic Jumping Spiders," in *Animal Cognition in Nature: The Convergence of Psychology and Biology in Laboratory and Field*, ed. Russell P. Balda, Irene M. Pepperberg, and Alan C. Kamil (San Diego: Academic, 1998), 411–34, quotation at 412.

46. See George J. Romanes, *Animal Intelligence* (London: Kegan Paul, Trench, & Co., 1882), 229.

47. See E. A. McMahan, "Bait-and-Capture Strategy of a Termite-Eating Assassin Bug," *Insectes Sociaux* (*Social Insects*) 29 (1982): 346–51.

48. See, for example, Romanes, 135–39.

49. See Griffin, 102.

50. See John S. Watson, *The Reasoning Power in Animals* (London: L. Reeve, 1867), 455.

51. See John Topham, "Ingenuity in a Spider," *Nature*, 5 Nov. 1874, 8.

52. See Romanes, 213.

53. See Wilcox and Jackson.

54. See Wilcox and Jackson.

55. Wilcox and Jackson, 425.

56. Wilcox and Jackson, 423.

57. Wilcox and Jackson, 423.

58. See Donald E. Landenberger, "Learning in the Pacific Starfish *Pisaster giganteus*," *Animal Behaviour* 14 (1966): 414–18, quotation at 414.

9 Nonspeciesist Law

1. Tom Regan, *The Case for Animal Rights* (Berkeley: University of California Press, 1983), 394.

2. For an actual case, see Gavin Daws, "'Animal Liberation' as Crime: The Hawaii Dolphin Case," in *Ethics and Animals*, ed. Harlan B. Miller and William H. Williams (Clifton, N.J.: Humana, 1983), 361–71; *State v. LeVasseur*, 613 Pacific Reporter, 2d ser., 1328–35 (Hawaii Appellate Court 1980). For a hypothetical case, see Lee Hall and Anthony Jon Waters, "From Property to Person: The Case of Evelyn Hart," *Seton Hall Constitutional Law Journal* 11, no. 1 (2000): 1–68.

3. See *Superintendent of Belchertown v. Saikewicz*, 370 North Eastern Reporter, 2d ser., 417–35 (Mass. Supreme Court 1977); *Youngberg v. Romeo*, 457 U.S. Reports 307–31 (1982). Also see the discussion on pages 107–8 of this book.

4. See Joyce S. Tischler, "Rights for Nonhuman Animals: A Guardianship Model for Dogs and Cats," *San Diego Law Review* 14, no. 2 (1977): 484–506.

5. Gary L. Francione, *Introduction to Animal Rights: Your Child or the Dog?* (Philadelphia: Temple University Press, 2000), xxxi.

6. Paola Cavalieri, *The Animal Question: Why Nonhuman Animals Deserve Human Rights*, 2d ed., trans. Catherine Woollard (New York: Oxford University Press, 2001), 142.

7. Francione, *Introduction to Animal Rights*, xxviii.

8. Francione, *Introduction to Animal Rights*, 221 n. 3.

9. See *Miles v. City Council of Augusta, Georgia*, 710 Federal Reporter, 2d ser., 1542–44 (1983).

10. Gary L. Francione, "Wildlife and Animal Rights," in *Ethics and Wildlife*, ed. Priscilla Cohn (Lewiston, N.Y.: Edwin Mellen, 1999), 65–81, at 76.

11. For example, Francione, *Introduction to Animal Rights*, 100.

12. See Francione, *Introduction to Animal Rights*, 153–54.

13. Francione, *Introduction to Animal Rights*, 101.

14. See Steve F. Sapontzis, *Morals, Reason, and Animals* (Philadelphia: Temple University Press, 1987), 104.

15. Francione, "Wildlife and Animal Rights," 76.

16. See Francione, *Introduction to Animal Rights*, xxxi.

17. Francione, *Introduction to Animal Rights*, 165, 155.

18. Francione, *Introduction to Animal Rights*, xxxii.

19. Francione, *Introduction to Animal Rights*, 155.

20. Gary L. Francione, "Comparable Harm and Equal Inherent Value: The Problem of the Dog in the Lifeboat," *Between the Species*, Summer/Fall 1995, 81–89, at 87.

21. Francione, "Comparable Harm and Equal Inherent Value," 87.

22. See Cavalieri, 30.

23. See Cavalieri, 6–7.

24. Francione, "Wildlife and Animal Rights," 77.

25. Francione, "Wildlife and Animal Rights," 77.

26. See Gary L. Francione, *Animals, Property, and the Law* (Philadelphia: Temple University Press, 1995), 91–92.

27. Bernard E. Rollin, *Animal Rights and Human Morality*, 2d ed. (Buffalo, N.Y.: Prometheus, 1992), 104.

28. Francione, *Introduction to Animal Rights*, 184.

10 Nonspeciesist Advocacy

1. John Mackey quoted in Bruce Horovitz, "Whole Foods Pledges to Be More Humane," *USA Today*, 21 Oct. 2003, B1.

2. Priscilla Feral, "Open Letter to John Mackey, CEO, Whole Foods Market," 31 Oct. 2003.

3. See National Agricultural Statistics Service (NASS), *Livestock Slaughter: 2003 Summary*, Mar. 2004, 1; NASS, *Poultry Slaughter: 2003 Annual Summary*, Mar. 2004, 2–3; U.S. Census Bureau, *Census 2000 Basics* (Washington, D.C.: U.S. Government Printing Office, 2002), 1.

4. David Cantor quoted in John N. Frank, "Animal Rights vs. Industry Battle Moves to Campuses," *PRWeek*, 10 Nov. 2003, 5.

5. See Gavin Daws, "'Animal Liberation' as Crime: The Hawaii Dolphin Case," in *Ethics and Animals*, ed. Harlan B. Miller and William H. Williams (Clifton, N.J.: Humana, 1983), 361–71; *State v. LeVasseur*, 613 Pacific Reporter, 2d ser., 1328–35 (Hawaii Appellate Court 1980).

6. See *Superintendent of Belchertown v. Saikewicz*, 370 North Eastern Reporter,

2d ser., 417–35 (Mass. Supreme Court 1977); *Youngberg v. Romeo*, 457 U.S. Reports 307–31 (1982). Also see the discussion on pages 107–8 of this book.

7. For detailed guidelines on nonspeciesist language, see Joan Dunayer, *Animal Equality: Language and Liberation* (Derwood, Md.: Ryce, 2001).

Select Bibliography

Animal Rights Theory

Cavalieri, Paola. *The Animal Question: Why Nonhuman Animals Deserve Human Rights*. 2d ed. Translated by Catherine Woollard. New York: Oxford University Press, 2001.

Cavalieri, Paola, and Peter Singer. "The Great Ape Project—and Beyond." In *The Great Ape Project: Equality beyond Humanity*, edited by Paola Cavalieri and Peter Singer, 304–12. New York: St. Martin's, 1993.

Cavalieri, Paola, Peter Singer, et al. "A Declaration on Great Apes." In *The Great Ape Project: Equality beyond Humanity*, edited by Paola Cavalieri and Peter Singer, 4–7. New York: St. Martin's, 1993.

Dunayer, Joan. *Animal Equality: Language and Liberation*. Derwood, Md.: Ryce, 2001.

Francione, Gary L. *Animals, Property, and the Law*. Philadelphia: Temple University Press, 1995.

———. "Comparable Harm and Equal Inherent Value: The Problem of the Dog in the Lifeboat." *Between the Species*, Summer/Fall 1995, 81–89.

———. *Introduction to Animal Rights: Your Child or the Dog?* Philadelphia: Temple University Press, 2000.

———. "Personhood, Property and Legal Competence." In *The Great Ape Project: Equality beyond Humanity*, edited by Paola Cavalieri and Peter Singer, 248–57. New York: St. Martin's, 1993.

———. *Rain without Thunder: The Ideology of the Animal Rights Movement*. Philadelphia: Temple University Press, 1996.

———. "Wildlife and Animal Rights." In *Ethics and Wildlife*, edited by Priscilla Cohn, 65–81. Lewiston, N.Y.: Edwin Mellen, 1999.

Hall, Lee, and Anthony Jon Waters. "From Property to Person: The Case of Evelyn Hart." *Seton Hall Constitutional Law Journal* 11, no. 1 (2000): 1–68.

Nibert, David. *Animal Rights/Human Rights: Entanglements of Oppression and Liberation.* Lanham, Md.: Rowman & Littlefield, 2002.

Pluhar, Evelyn B. *Beyond Prejudice: The Moral Significance of Human and Nonhuman Animals.* Durham, N.C.: Duke University Press, 1995.

Rachels, James. *Created from Animals: The Moral Implications of Darwinism.* Oxford: Oxford University Press, 1990.

Regan, Tom. *The Case for Animal Rights.* Berkeley: University of California Press, 1983.

———. "The Case for Animal Rights." In *The Animal Rights Debate*, by Carl Cohen and Tom Regan, 125–222. Lanham, Md.: Rowman & Littlefield, 2001.

Rollin, Bernard. *Animal Rights and Human Morality.* 2d ed. Buffalo, N.Y.: Prometheus, 1992.

Rowlands, Mark. *Animals Like Us.* London: Verso, 2002.

Ryder, Richard. "An Autobiography." *Between the Species*, Summer 1992, 168–73.

Sapontzis, Steve F. "Aping Persons—Pro and Con." In *The Great Ape Project: Equality beyond Humanity*, edited by Paola Cavalieri and Peter Singer, 269–77. New York: St. Martin's, 1993.

———. *Morals, Reason, and Animals.* Philadelphia: Temple University Press, 1987.

Singer, Peter. "*Animal Equality: Language and Liberation* by Joan Dunayer" (book review). *Vegan Voice*, Dec. 2001–Feb. 2002, 36.

———. *Animal Liberation.* 2d ed. New York: New York Review of Books, 1990.

———. "Animal Liberation at 30." *New York Review of Books*, 15 May 2003, 23–26.

———. *Practical Ethics.* 2d ed. Cambridge: Cambridge University Press, 1993.

Tischler, Joyce S. "Rights for Nonhuman Animals: A Guardianship Model for Dogs and Cats." *San Diego Law Review* 14, no. 2 (1977): 484–506.

Wise, Steven M. *Drawing the Line: Science and the Case for Animal Rights.* Cambridge, Mass.: Perseus, 2002.

———. *Rattling the Cage: Toward Legal Rights for Animals.* Cambridge, Mass.: Perseus, 2000.

Wolfson, David J. *Beyond the Law: Agribusiness and the Systemic*

Abuse of Animals Raised for Food or Food Production. 2d ed. Watkins Glen, N.Y.: Farm Sanctuary, 1999.

Nonhuman Consciousness

American Society of Ichthyologists and Herpetologists, American Fisheries Society, and American Institute of Fisheries Research Biologists. "Guidelines for Use of Fishes in Field Research." *Fisheries* 13, no. 2 (1988): 16–23.

American Society of Ichthyologists and Herpetologists, Herpetologists' League, and Society for the Study of Amphibians and Reptiles. "Guidelines for Use of Live Amphibians and Reptiles in Field Research." ASIH website (http://www.asih.org/pubs/herpcoll.html), 28 Dec. 2002.

American Veterinary Medical Association. "2000 Report of the AVMA Panel on Euthanasia." *Journal of the American Veterinary Medical Association*, 1 Mar. 2001, 669–96.

Barber, Theodore X. *The Human Nature of Birds: A Scientific Discovery with Startling Implications.* New York: St. Martin's, 1993.

Beck, Benjamin B. *Animal Tool Behavior: The Use and Manufacture of Tools by Animals.* New York: Garland, 1980.

Broglio, Cristina, Fernando Rodríguez, and Cosme Salas. "Spatial Cognition and Its Neural Basis in Teleost Fishes." *Fish and Fisheries* 4, no. 3 (2003): 247–55.

Bshary, Redouan, Wolfgang Wickler, and Hans Fricke. "Fish Cognition: A Primate's Eye View." *Animal Cognition* 5, no. 1 (2002): 1–13.

Burton, Maurice. *Just Like an Animal.* New York: Charles Scribner's Sons, 1978.

Butler, Ann B., and William Hodos. *Comparative Vertebrate Neuroanatomy: Evolution and Adaptation.* New York: Wiley-Liss, 1996.

Davis, Hank, and Rachelle Pérusse, "Numerical Competence in Animals: Definitional Issues, Current Evidence, and a New Research Agenda." *Behavioral and Brain Sciences* 11, no. 4 (1988): 561–79, 611–15.

Deacon, Terrence W. "Rethinking Mammalian Brain Evolution." *American Zoologist* 30, no. 3 (1990): 629–705.

Dews, P. B. "Some Observations on an Operant in the Octopus."
Journal of the Experimental Analysis of Behavior 2, no. 1 (1959):
57–63.

Eisemann, C. H., et al. "Do Insects Feel Pain?—A Biological View."
Experientia (now *Cellular and Molecular Life Sciences*) 40 (1984):
164–67.

Fiorito, Graziano. "Is There 'Pain' in Invertebrates?" *Behavioural
Processes* 12 (1986): 383–88.

Giurfa, Martin, et al. "The Concepts of 'Sameness' and 'Difference'
in an Insect." *Nature*, 19 Apr. 2001, 930–33.

Gonzalez, Philip, and Leonore Fleischer. *The Dog Who Rescues
Cats: The True Story of Ginny*. New York: HarperCollins, 1995.

Gould, James L. "Natural History of Honey Bee Learning." In *The
Biology of Learning*, edited by Peter Marler and Herbert S. Terrace, 149–80. Berlin: Springer, 1984.

Gould, James L., and Carol Grant Gould. *The Honey Bee*. New
York: Scientific American Library, 1988.

Griffin, Donald R. *Animal Minds*. Chicago: University of Chicago
Press, 1992.

"Habits and Intelligence of *Vespa maculata*." *Proceedings of the
Academy of Natural Sciences of Philadelphia*, 22 Jan. 1878, 15.

Harrison, Laura M., et al. "The Opiate System in Invertebrates."
Peptides 15, no. 7 (1994): 1309–29.

Huntingford, Felicity. "Foreword." *Fish and Fisheries* 4, no. 3 (2003):
197–98.

Kaufman, Kenn. "The Subject Is Alex." *Audubon*, Sept./Oct. 1991,
52–58.

Kavaliers, Martin. "Evolutionary and Comparative Aspects of Nociception." *Brain Research Bulletin* 21, no. 6 (1988): 923–31.

Kelley, Jennifer L., and Anne E. Magurran. "Learned Predator Recognition and Antipredator Responses in Fishes." *Fish and Fisheries* 4, no. 3 (2003): 216–26.

Kestin, Steve C. *Pain and Stress in Fish*. Horsham, England: Royal
Society for the Prevention of Cruelty to Animals, 1994.

Kirby, Alex. "Parrot's Oratory Stuns Scientists." *BBC News Online*
(http://news.bbc.co.uk), 26 Jan. 2004.

Laland, Kevin N., Culum Brown, and Jens Krause. "Learning in
Fishes: From Three-Second Memory to Culture." *Fish and Fisheries* 4, no. 3 (2003): 199–202.

Landenberger, Donald E. "Learning in the Pacific Starfish *Pisaster giganteus.*" *Animal Behaviour* 14 (1966): 414–18.

Langworthy, Ronald A., and Joseph W. Jennings. "Odd Ball, Abstract, Olfactory Learning in Laboratory Rats." *Psychological Record* 22, no. 4 (1972): 487–90.

Machin, Karen L. "Fish, Amphibian, and Reptile Analgesia." *Veterinary Clinics of North America: Exotic Animal Practice* 4, no. 1 (2001): 19–33.

Marler, Peter. "Social Cognition: Are Primates Smarter than Birds?" *Current Ornithology* 13 (1996): 1–32.

Masserman, Jules H., Stanley Wechkin, and William Terris. "'Altruistic' Behavior in Rhesus Monkeys." *American Journal of Psychiatry* 121 (1964): 584–85.

Masson, Jeffrey M., and Susan McCarthy. *When Elephants Weep: The Emotional Lives of Animals.* New York: Delacorte, 1995.

McMahan, E. A. "Bait-and-Capture Strategy of a Termite-Eating Assassin Bug." *Insectes Sociaux (Social Insects)* 29 (1982): 346–51.

Menzel, Randolf, and Martin Giurfa. "Cognitive Architecture of a Mini-Brain: The Honeybee." *Trends in Cognitive Sciences* 5, no. 2 (2001): 62–71.

Menzel, Randolf, et al. "Biology of Invertebrate Learning: Group Report." In *The Biology of Learning*, edited by Peter Marler and Herbert S. Terrace, 249–70. Berlin: Springer, 1984.

Newall, R. S. "Carnivorous Wasps." *Nature*, 25 Mar. 1880, 494.

Patterson, Francine, and Eugene Linden. *The Education of Koko.* New York: Holt, Rinehart & Winston, 1981.

Pepperberg, Irene M. "Numerical Competence in an African Gray Parrot (*Psittacus erithacus*)." *Journal of Comparative Psychology* 108, no. 1 (1994): 36–44.

Pepperberg, Irene M., and Michael V. Brezinsky. "Acquisition of a Relative Class Concept by an African Gray Parrot (*Psittacus erithacus*): Discriminations Based on Relative Size." *Journal of Comparative Psychology* 105, no. 3 (1991): 286–94.

Premack, David, and Ann J. Premack. *The Mind of an Ape.* New York: W. W. Norton, 1983.

Romanes, George J. *Animal Intelligence.* London: Kegan Paul, Trench, & Co., 1882.

Rose, Margaret, and David Adams. "Evidence for Pain and Suffering in Other Animals." In *Animal Experimentation: The Consensus*

Changes, edited by Gill Langley, 42–71. New York: Macmillan, 1989.

Ryden, Hope. *Lily Pond: Four Years with a Family of Beavers*. New York: William Morrow, 1989.

Sahley, Christie L. "Behavior Theory and Invertebrate Learning." In *The Biology of Learning*, edited by Peter Marler and Herbert S. Terrace, 181–96. Berlin: Springer, 1984.

Sahley, Christie L., and Donald F. Ready. "Associative Learning Modifies Two Behaviors in the Leech, *Hirudo medicinalis*." *Journal of Neuroscience* 8, no. 12 (1988): 4612–20.

Schusterman, Ronald J., and Kathy Krieger. "Artificial Language Comprehension and Size Transposition by a California Sea Lion (*Zalophus californianus*)." *Journal of Comparative Psychology* 100, no. 4 (1986): 348–55.

Smith, Jane A., and Kenneth M. Boyd, eds. "Pain, Stress, and Anxiety in Animals." Chapter 4 in *Lives in the Balance: The Ethics of Using Animals in Biomedical Research*, 45–77. Oxford: Oxford University Press, 1991.

Sneddon, Lynne U. "The Evidence for Pain in Fish: The Use of Morphine as an Analgesic." *Applied Animal Behaviour Science* 83, no. 2 (2003): 153–62.

Sneddon, Lynne U., Victoria A. Braithwaite, and Michael J. Gentle. "Do Fishes Have Nociceptors? Evidence for the Evolution of a Vertebrate Sensory System." *Proceedings of the Royal Society of London: Series B* 270, no. 1520 (2003): 1115–22.

Sosin, Mark, and John Clark. *Through the Fish's Eye: An Angler's Guide to Gamefish Behavior*. New York: Harper & Row, 1973.

Topham, John. "Ingenuity in a Spider." *Nature*, 5 Nov. 1874, 8.

van Swinderen, Bruno, and Ralph J. Greenspan. "Salience Modulates 20–30 Hz Brain Activity in *Drosophila*." *Nature Neuroscience* 6, no. 6 (2003): 579–86.

Waddell, Scott, and William G. Quinn. "Flies, Genes, and Learning." *Annual Review of Neuroscience* 24 (2001): 1283–1309.

Warburton, Kevin. "Learning of Foraging Skills by Fish." *Fish and Fisheries* 4, no. 3 (2003): 203–15.

Wigglesworth, V. B. "Do Insects Feel Pain?" *Antenna* 4 (1980): 8–9.

Wilcox, R. Stimson, and Robert R. Jackson. "Cognitive Abilities of Araneophagic Jumping Spiders." In *Animal Cognition in Nature: The Convergence of Psychology and Biology in Laboratory and*

Field, edited by Russell P. Balda, Irene M. Pepperberg, and Alan C. Kamil, 411–34. San Diego: Academic, 1998.

Wodinsky, Erika, R. Behrend, and M. E. Bitterman. "Avoidance Conditioning in Two Species of Fish." *Animal Behaviour* 10, no. 1 (1962): 76–78.

Index

invertebrates
abuse of, 42, 45, 47
consciousness of, 92, 126–34
See also insects; octopuses
involuntary servitude, concept of,
35, 45, 136
IQ (intelligence quotient), basic
rights and, 25–26, 89, 90, 107–8,
123, 159

jellyfishes, sentience of, 127, 129
See also invertebrates
Jews. *See* anti-Semitism and spe-
ciesism, parallels between
Judeo-Christianity and speciesism,
11–12, 15–16, 57, 61
Justice for All Species (JAS), 158

KFC (formerly Kentucky Fried
Chicken), 61, 154
kidnapping of nonhumans, 45, 138,
140–41, 147
killer whales. *See* orcas in aquaprisons
kinship, denial of human–
nonhuman, xi, 9, 12
Koko (gorilla), 26
kosher slaughter, 47
Krause, Jens, 80
Ku Klux Klan (KKK), 10, 57

Laland, Kevin, 80
language ability in nonhumans
human-language ability, 21, 26,
86–87, 109
natural communication, 23, 24–
25, 85, 103–4, 131
language, racist, 99, 107
language, sexist, xi, 54, 99, 107

language, speciesist, xi, 51, 54, 72–
73, 107
animal, xi, 12, 56, 57, 160
category labels, exploitive, xiii,
13, 18–19, 55–57, 72, 160
erasure of nonhumans, 37
euphemisms, xii–xiii, 54–55,
56, 72, 158
hierarchical language, 11, 57,
106
individuality, denial of nonhuman, xii, 13–14, 33, 34
oxymorons, xiii, 56
plural nonhuman terms, xii
pronoun use, xii, 12, 56, 160
separate vocabularies for nonhumans and humans, 73, 158
trivializing of nonhuman suffering and death, 51, 57
"welfarist" language, xiii, 56, 57
law, new-speciesist, 99, 100–111
See also new-speciesist advocacy; new-speciesist philosophy
law, nonspeciesist, 137–49
See also legal rights, nonhuman;
nonspeciesist philosophy
law, old-speciesist, 31, 48–49
Animal Welfare Act, 41–45, 49,
64–65, 138
cruelty statutes, 31, 32, 35–41,
43, 49, 63, 138
Humane Methods of Slaughter
Act, 45–48, 49, 64, 65, 138
"wildlife conservation" laws,
33–35, 49, 117
See also property status of nonhumans
laws, "animal." *See* law, old-
speciesist
laying hens. *See* egg industry,
cruelty of

New Jersey Animal Rights
Alliance (NJARA), 158
new speciesism, meaning of, 77, 98
new-speciesist advocacy, 113–20
    See also law, new-speciesist;
    new-speciesist philosophy
new-speciesist criteria for rights
    complexity, 88–90, 92, 95, 114,
    115
    desire to stay alive, 81–84, 92
    emotionality, 92, 113, 115–16
    genetic closeness to humans,
    104–5, 115, 116, 118
    human-like behavior, 106, 115
    individuality, rich, 78, 114
    intelligence, human-like, 86–90,
    101, 106–7, 113, 115–16
    self-awareness, 79–81, 86, 91,
    92–93, 101, 102, 115
    sociability, 84, 91, 115
    See also new-speciesist phi-
    losophy
new-speciesist law. *See* law, new-
    speciesist
new-speciesist philosophy, 77
    Cavalieri, 114–15, 118
    Francione, 95–96, 115–16, 124,
    143–46
    Pluhar, 92, 94–95, 96
    Rachels, 86, 87, 88–89, 90, 114
    Regan, 91–94, 95, 96–98
    Rowlands, 83, 87, 90, 97
    Singer, 77–86, 87, 90, 91, 114–
    15, 118
    See also new-speciesist criteria
    for rights; Wise, Steven
Nibert, David, 5, 61, 64, 65
N'kisi (African gray parrot), 87
nonhuman (the term), xi, xii
nonspeciesist advocacy. *See* advo-
    cacy, nonspeciesist
nonspeciesist law. *See* law, non-
    speciesist

nonspeciesist, meaning of, 124, 134
    See also speciesism, meaning of
nonspeciesist philosophy, 123–26,
    134

octopuses, 42, 105, 128, 129–30
old speciesism, meaning of, 9
    See also speciesism, meaning of
old speciesism, rationalizations for
    contract argument, 16–17
    individuality, human, 12–15
    intelligence, human, 22–26
    morality, human, 26–30
    preference for humans, 9–11
    religious beliefs, 11–12, 15–16
    suffering, human, 19–22
    value of human life, 17–19
old-speciesist advocacy. *See* advo-
    cacy, old-speciesist
old-speciesist law. *See* law, old-
    speciesist
old-speciesist philosophy. *See* old
    speciesism, rationalizations for
opiates and nonhumans, 20, 128
orangutans, 12, 44–45, 78, 87, 102
    See also great apes
orcas in aquaprisons, 42
orthonectids and insentience, 126
Ota Benga, 44–45
overpopulation, human, 14–15, 19,
    144, 146
oxymorons, speciesist, xiii, 56

pain, nonhuman, 19–21, 127–29
parakeets, 21–22, 41
    See also birds
parasites, 125, 126, 135, 148
parrots. *See* African gray parrots;
    birds; parakeets
pelt industry, 21, 35, 36, 40, 49,
    137

People for the Ethical Treatment of
Animals (PETA), 59–60, 61, 63,
72
Pepperberg, Irene, 109
perceptual powers of nonhumans,
23, 25, 89, 95
personhood, nonhuman
legal, 99–100, 137–42, 147,
158–59
moral, xii, 79, 88, 91
See also legal rights, nonhuman;
property status of nonhumans;
sentience as appropriate basis
for rights
"pest control," 39, 141, 142
pet (the term), 55–56
pet industry, 41–42, 44
See also breeding of nonhumans, immorality of human;
inbreeding, effects of
pets, legal status of, 31–33, 39, 41–
42
phylogenetic scale, 88, 93, 102
See also evolution; hierarchy,
speciesist
pigeons, cognition of, 21, 25–26,
86, 89
See also birds
pig-flesh industry, cruelty of, 10,
22, 35–36, 47–48, 59
placozoans and insentience, 126
plants and insentience, 127
Pluhar, Evelyn, 84, 92, 94–95, 96
plural nonhuman terms, xii
polar bears, 34, 43
pork industry. *See* pig-flesh
industry, cruelty of
poultry (the term), 55, 56–57, 160
poultry industry. *See* bird-flesh industry, cruelty of; egg industry,
cruelty of; fatty-bird-liver industry
prairie dogs, communication in, 25

praying mantises, sentience of, 128
See also insects
precautionary principle of law, 107
predation and morality, 26–27, 29,
125, 148
primates, 12, 64–65
See also great apes; monkeys,
abuse of
product testing on rabbits, 14
pronoun use, speciesist, xii, 12, 56,
160
property, nonhuman right to, 142–47
property status of nonhumans, 31,
48
and abolitionism versus "welfarism," 51, 63, 69, 70, 152
as construct, 11, 17
federal laws and, 34, 41, 44, 45,
49, 64–65
immorality of, 49, 124, 136, 139
legally challenging the, 99–100,
137–38, 158–59
state laws and, 31–33, 35, 38, 41
See also enslavement, parallels
between African-American
and nonhuman; personhood,
nonhuman
protoctists and insentience, 127
puppy mills, 41–42
pygmy chimpanzees. *See* bonobos

rabbits in vivisection, 14
Rachels, James, 86–87, 88–90, 92,
114
racing, dog, 19
racing, horse, 19, 36
racism and speciesism, parallels
between, 1–2, 3–4, 10, 19, 30, 88
See also anti-Semitism and speciesism, parallels between;
blacks, parallels between spe-